Armies of the Normans, 911–1194

Armies of the Normans, 911–1194

Organization, Equipment and Tactics

Gabriele Esposito

Pen & Sword
MILITARY

First published in Great Britain in 2024
by Pen & Sword Military
An imprint of
Pen & Sword Books Limited
Yorkshire – Philadelphia

Copyright © Gabriele Esposito 2024

ISBN 978 1 39904 740 1

The right of Gabriele Esposito to be identified as
Author of this Work has been asserted by him in accordance
with the Copyright, Designs and Patents Act 1988.

A CIP catalogue record for this book is
available from the British Library

All rights reserved. No part of this book may be reproduced or
transmitted in any form or by any means, electronic or mechanical
including photocopying, recording or by any information storage and
retrieval system, without permission from the Publisher in writing.

Typeset by Mac Style
Printed and bound in India by Replika Press Pvt. Ltd.

Pen & Sword Books Limited incorporates the imprints of After the Battle,
Atlas, Archaeology, Aviation, Discovery, Family History, Fiction, History,
Maritime, Military, Military Classics, Politics, Select, Transport, True Crime,
Air World, Frontline Publishing, Leo Cooper, Remember When, Seaforth
Publishing, The Praetorian Press, Wharncliffe Local History, Wharncliffe
Transport, Wharncliffe True Crime and White Owl.

For a complete list of Pen & Sword titles please contact

PEN & SWORD BOOKS LIMITED
47 Church Street, Barnsley, South Yorkshire, S70 2AS, England
E-mail: enquiries@pen-and-sword.co.uk
Website: www.pen-and-sword.co.uk
or
PEN AND SWORD BOOKS
1950 Lawrence Rd, Havertown, PA 19083, USA
E-mail: uspen-and-sword@casematepublishers.com
Website: www.penandswordbooks.com

Contents

Acknowledgements		vii
Introduction		viii
Chapter 1	The Origins of the Normans	1
Chapter 2	The Duchy of Normandy	21
Chapter 3	The Norman Conquest of England	32
Chapter 4	The Reign of William the Conqueror	48
Chapter 5	Norman England Under William II and Henry I	59
Chapter 6	The Norman Conquest of Southern Italy	72
Chapter 7	The Norman Contribution to the First Crusade	86
Chapter 8	The Norman Kingdom of Sicily	123
Chapter 9	Norman Military Organization and Equipment	134
Bibliography		150
The Re-enactors who Contributed to this Book		151
Index		154

Gabriele Esposito is a military historian who works as a freelance author and researcher for some of the most important publishing houses in the military history sector. In particular, he is an expert specializing in uniformology: his interests and expertise range from the ancient civilizations to modern post-colonial conflicts. During recent years he has conducted and published several researches on the military history of the Latin American countries, with special attention on the War of the Triple Alliance and the War of the Pacific. He is among the leading experts on the military history of the Italian Wars of Unification and the Spanish Carlist Wars. His books and essays are published on a regular basis by Pen & Sword Books, Osprey Publishing, Winged Hussar Publishing and Libreria Editrice Goriziana, and he is also the author of numerous military history articles appearing in specialized magazines such as *Ancient Warfare Magazine*, *Medieval Warfare Magazine*, *The Armourer*, *History of War*, *Guerres et Histoire*, *Focus Storia* and *Focus Storia Wars*.

Acknowledgements

This book is dedicated to my magnificent parents, Maria Rosaria and Benedetto, for the immense love and fundamental support that they always give me. Thanks to their precious advice, over many years, this book has turned out even better than I had envisaged. A very special thanks goes to Philip Sidnell, the commissioning editor of my books for Pen & Sword: his love for history and his passion for publishing are the key factors behind the success of our publications. Many thanks also to the production manager of this title, Matt Jones, for his excellent work and great enthusiasm. A special mention is due to Tony Walton, for the magnificent work of editing that he makes for all my books. A very special mention goes to the brilliant re-enactment groups that collaborated with their photos to the creation of this book: without the incredible work of research of their members, the final result of this publication would have not been the same. As a result, I want to express my deep gratitude to the following living history associations: Historia Aquitanorum, De Gueules et d'Argent, Milites Pagenses and Les Guerriers du Moyen-Age from France, and Sussex Medieval Society from the United Kingdom.

Introduction

The Normans were some of the most effective military fighters of the Middle Ages, their great martial abilities gaining them two major realms in a turbulent historical period that was characterized by great political fragmentation throughout Europe. The Normans are generally considered the perfect representation of the iconic feudal knight, a professional soldier equipped with full armour and fighting as a heavy cavalryman. It should be remembered, however, that the feudal military system based on the prominence of armoured cavalry was not created by the Normans: it was introduced by Charlemagne and by his Carolingian successors, but it was the Normans who interpreted and formalized it in the most effective way. Compared to all the other fighters of their age, the Normans had a somewhat different nature due to their peculiar ethnic origins. As we will see, they were the heirs of Viking raiders who settled in northern France during the tenth century and gave their name to the region today known as Normandy. The Normans always retained the impressive military *furor*, or fury, of their Scandinavian ancestors, but soon transformed themselves from pirates into feudal warlords. They became the most powerful vassals of the King of France and adopted the military institutions of feudalism in full, learning from their former enemies. The Normans transformed themselves from foot warriors armed with axes to heavily armoured knights trained to charge in close order with spear and shield. They were superior to the other feudal knights of France, and thus their leaders started to play a prominent role in the politics of the French realm. The Norman knights, or *milites*, had the best military equipment of their age: nasal helmet, chainmail, kite shield and longsword. They rode the best horses of continental Europe and learned how to fight on horseback during childhood. Thanks to the use of stirrups and saddles with tall pommels, a Norman knight could enjoy a high degree of stability while fighting on horseback and could charge with his spear tucked under the armpit, which enabled him to hit his targets with the full kinetic energy derived from his horse's speed. No enemy infantryman, armoured or not, could resist the charge of the Norman *milites*, who usually attacked in small tactical groups of between twenty and twenty-five knights, known as a *conrois*, which were deployed on the battlefield in a wedge formation. Thanks to their military superiority, the Normans started to expand their territorial domains in northern France and be employed as mercenaries across the Mediterranean. In the following chapters we will follow the Normans in their incredible campaigns of conquest, which had enormous success. We will see how the most famous Duke of Normandy, William the Conqueror, invaded the Kingdom of England in 1066 and progressively transformed it into the most important Norman realm in Europe. We will also detail the Norman conquest of southern Italy, which saw the northern adventurers fighting against a huge variety of Mediterranean enemies, their successes enabling them to unify a large portion of Italy as the Kingdom of Sicily, which remained a powerful Norman state until the end of the twelfth century. One chapter will explain why the First Crusade came to be considered as a Norman enterprise and how two Norman warlords from southern Italy distinguished themselves in the Christian conquest of the Levant. The final chapter will present an overview of the Normans' military organization and equipment in order to show why they were so effective and feared on the battlefields of the age.

Chapter 1

The Origins of the Normans

Broadly speaking, the Normans were the direct heirs of the Viking raiders who during the early tenth century settled in the region of north-eastern France today known as Normandy. To understand the true nature of the Normans, it is therefore necessary to consider the main causes that determined the expansion of the Vikings across Europe during the Middle Ages. In several European countries, the terms 'Vikings' and 'Normans' are commonly used to identify those Scandinavian raiders who operated across Europe during the period from 800–1000. However, it should be noted that all the Vikings belonged to the larger group of the Norsemen, a north Germanic ethno-linguistic group that spoke the Old Norse language and lived in the southern part of Scandinavia. Their homeland comprised present-day Denmark as well as the southern parts of Norway and Sweden. From a cultural point of view, the Norsemen had a lot in common with the south Germanic tribes who invaded the Roman Empire during the last centuries of Antiquity. Unlike the southern Germani, however, they always had very little contact with the most advanced civilizations of Continental or Mediterranean Europe, such as the Celts or the Romans. Consequently, the material culture of the Norsemen was quite primitive compared to the more civilized Europeans from the Mediterranean area. In many aspects, the Norsemen had remained at an earlier phase in the evolution process that had transformed the Germani of the south into an advanced civilization. But like the earlier south Germanic tribes, the Norsemen were skilled warriors and lived in small rural villages; they knew how to work metals in order to produce formidable weapons but did not practice agriculture on a large scale. Their lands were difficult to reach for foreign merchants and the natural environment in which they lived was particularly harsh, which combined to make their economy very simple with no monetary system. During the long centuries of the Roman Empire, their only direct contact with the regions of southern Europe was through the trading of amber, a precious material that could be found only in the Baltic Sea. The Norsemen thus knew very little of the rest of the world, and were too few to represent a driving force in the new world that was emerging from the end of Antiquity.

Over time, however, this situation started to change very rapidly, and an increasing number of Norsemen began to leave their homeland in order to travel abroad in

Norman knight equipped with sword and kite shield.
(*Photo and copyright by Historia Aquitanorum*)

Norman knights, both wearing a variation of the famous nasal helmet. (*Photo and copyright by Historia Aquitanorum*)

search of new lands to raid or to colonize. Those Norsemen who abandoned their previous lifestyle to become pirates and explorers started to be known as Vikings; as a result, we can say that all the Vikings were Norsemen, but that only some Norsemen were Vikings. The expansion of the Norsemen across northern Europe began during the closing decades of the eighth century, in an age that saw the ascendancy of the Frankish Empire in Continental Europe and the end of Arab expansionism across the Mediterranean. The reasons that determined the emergence of the Vikings are many and varied, and are still a matter of discussion among modern scholars. Whatever the truth, each of these reasons played a part in causing a radical change in the traditional society of the Norsemen. Before the beginning of the so-called Viking Age, southern Scandinavia underwent a great demographic expansion that was mostly caused by climatic changes. Until the middle of the eighth century, the climate of countries like Denmark or Norway was too cold to permit the existence of a large population, significantly limiting agricultural production. By 750, this situation had started to change, the climate becoming less cold and the population henceforth starting to expand due to an increased production of food supplies. Within just a few decades, the demographic situation of Scandinavia changed dramatically, to the point that the region began experiencing problems relating to over-population. The agricultural capacity of the land was not enough to keep up with the increasing population, so many Norsemen found themselves without means of sustainment. The number of individuals who had no land and no personal properties increased, especially after all the cultivable lands had already been occupied. The sudden demographic boom produced a mass of landless men who were in search of material wealth in order to feed their families or of new territories where to settle as farmers. These individuals had no choice but to leave their homeland in search of new opportunities, operating as pirates or crossing the seas as explorers. Differently from the southern Germanic communities, the Norsemen were skilled navigators and knew how to build the most effective ships of the Middle Ages, so travelling long distances over the ocean or following the course of rivers for thousands of miles was not a problem for them.

While the demographic boom was undoubtedly the primary reason behind Viking expansionism, several other changes also took place in Scandinavia during the eighth century. First of all, iron became more common in the region due to the opening of new mines where this important material could be extracted. The new and increasing amounts of iron were then used to produce more effective weapons, as well as new agricultural tools that augmented the productivity of the Norse farmers. In addition, during those same years, the Norsemen improved their sea-faring capabilities by perfecting the design of their ships, with larger sails introduced together with new tacking practices. Thanks to these innovations and the fact that they learned how to sail at night by following the stars, the Norsemen could start planning ambitious raids and expeditions. When the Viking Age began, no central government existed in the three Scandinavian countries of Denmark, Sweden and Norway: each tribal group had its supreme leader and thus there was no political entity that could centrally control Viking expansionism. All the Norsemen were still pagans, with the Christian faith not yet practiced north of Charlemagne's domains. When the Vikings started launching their first raids, their primary target in the west was the British Isles, since most of Continental Europe was under the firm military control of the Carolingians, who had a very strong military apparatus and a centralized administration that could effectively defend their territory.

The military and political situation of Britain and Ireland, was completely different, being characterized by widespread fragmentation. England was populated by the

The Origins of the Normans 5

Norman knight equipped with nasal helmet.
(*Photo and copyright by Historia Aquitanorum*)

Norman knights bearing kite shields. (*Photo and copyright by Historia Aquitanorum*)

Anglo-Saxons, who had crossed the Channel some centuries before and created their own small realms after crushing the resistance of the Romano-British communities. For several decades, until Alfred the Great unified the country in 886, England was divided into seven small kingdoms that were constantly at war against each other and were collectively known as the Heptarchy: East Anglia, Mercia, Northumbria, Wessex, Essex, Kent and Sussex. The Vikings were well aware that these kingdoms were very weak militarily if attacked individually, and thus always nurtured an ambition to eventually conquer the whole of England. By conquering England, a very rich land, full of natural resources and perfect for agriculture, the Scandinavians could have resolved all their problems related to over-population. To the west of Anglo-Saxon England there were the small Celtic realms of Wales, which had been able to stop the expansionism of the Saxons during the previous decades but which were too fragmented politically to represent a significant military entity. By around 780, there were five main princedoms in Wales: Gwynedd, Powys, Dyfed, Gwent and Dumnonia. These were all inhabited by the direct heirs of the Romano-British communities who fought against the Saxons in England, and had a distinctive culture. To the north of the Heptarchy there was Scotland, which had long been inhabited by a confederation of Celtic peoples who were known as Picts. These had been at war with the Romans for many decades and had launched several devastating raids across England. The leading group among the Picts was the Fortriu, who dominated the other minor communities. There were, however, two smaller and independent kingdoms on the territory of present-day western Scotland that were not controlled by the Picts: the Kingdom of Dál Riata and the Kingdom of Strathclyde. The former was inhabited by Scoti coming from Ireland, while the latter was populated by Britons who had a lot in common with the Celtic communities of Wales. Compared with the Anglo-Saxons of England, however, the Picts were less fragmented from a political point of view, since they controlled most of Scotland. Ireland was inhabited by the Scoti or Gaels, another confederation of Celtic peoples who had a lot in common with the Picts. Over time, the original alliance existing between the Scoti and the Picts was destroyed by internal rivalries and the establishment of the Kingdom of Dál Riata in western Scotland, which led to several conflicts between the two communities. The Scoti of Ireland were extremely fragmented politically, their clans being organized as independent princedoms that were constantly at war against each other. There were six small realms in Ireland by the beginning of the Viking raids: Munster, Leinster, Connacht, Airgialla, Uí Néill and Ulaid. Like the Anglo-Saxon states of the Heptarchy, these were frequently ravaged by civil wars, with one of them occasionally emerging as a regional power.

Together with the British Isles, France was one of the main targets of the Scandinavian raids during the two centuries of the Viking Age. Present-day Normandy, in particular, was greatly exposed to the attacks of the Scandinavians due to its peculiar geographical position; being a peninsula stretching from northern France towards southern England, it was a perfect location for Viking naval bases. Normandy's name derives from Northmannia, a term that can be translated as Land of the Norsemen. When the Scandinavian incursions in France began, the latter country was still part of the mighty Carolingian Empire that had been created by Charlemagne. At the height of its power, the Frankish Empire dominated most of Continental Europe: from Catalonia in northern Spain to the lands of the Frisians in the Netherlands, from Brittany in north-western France to the heart of Germany. Charlemagne, one of the Middle Ages' greatest military leaders, died in early 814, having transformed Europe during his long reign, uniting most of the Germanic kingdoms that had emerged from the collapse of the Roman Empire into a single political entity. The great monarch was succeeded by his son Louis the Pious, who was able to preserve the unity of the Carolingian Empire despite the emergence of the Vikings and the outbreak of various bloody civil wars within the Frankish world. When Louis the Pious died in 840, a new internecine conflict broke out between his three sons, each of whom wanted to become emperor and had no intention of renouncing his claims. The hostilities came to an end only in the summer of

843, when the Treaty of Verdun was signed between the three pretenders to the Carolingian throne. According to the treaty's terms, the vast Frankish Empire was divided into three new states: West Francia, Middle Francia and East Francia. West Francia, roughly corresponding to present-day France, was given to Charles the Bald; Middle Francia, comprising the Rhineland and northern Italy, was assigned to Lothair I, who also inherited the imperial title; and East Francia, comprising most of western Germany, became the kingdom of Louis the German. The three new states had differing destinies. West Francia gradually became the Kingdom of France, while East Francia later became the Holy Roman Empire. The lands of Middle Francia, meanwhile, ceased to be autonomous in 870 when the Treaty of Meerssen partitioned them between Charles the Bald and Louis the German. Due to the frequent civil wars and many territorial changes during the period from 840–870, the territories of the former Carolingian Empire became extremely weak from a military point of view. This greatly helped the Vikings, who could attack the individual Frankish communities without having to face large combined armies. Most of the Scandinavian raids conducted in mainland Europe had as their target the emerging Kingdom of France or West Francia. Some early Viking incursions in France took place during the very last years of Charlemagne's reign, but it was under Charles the Bald that they became a significant problem for the French monarchy. The first recorded Scandinavian attack in France took place during 799, and was soon followed by a few others. In response to these early raids, around 810, Charlemagne stablished a form of coastal defence in the northern regions of his empire, but this was never fully implemented. In 820, during the reign of his son, Louis the Pious, a major Scandinavian incursion was repulsed at the mouth of the River Seine. In 834, the Vikings launched a new attack against Frisia, on the territory of the present-day Netherlands, which achieved much greater success. The following years saw an escalation of raids, with Antwerp, Rouen and Nantes all attacked by the Scandinavians, exploiting the weakness of the Frankish military system, which was heavily involved in the ongoing internecine conflicts.

In March 845, a large fleet of Danish Vikings, with 120 warships, entered the River Seine under the command of Ragnar Lodbrok. The target of the Scandinavian raiders was Paris, one of the richest cities of West Francia, of which it had been the capital since 987. Charles the Bald, determined to fight to the death in order to defend the city, quickly mobilized his military forces, dividing them into two parts, one deployed on the eastern bank of the Seine and the other on the western bank. At that time, Paris was still relatively small, not extending beyond the Ile de la Cité, a natural island in the middle of the Seine. After defeating one of the two Frankish armies and killing all the captured enemies in order to spread terror, Ragnar and his

Norman knight with pointed nasal helmet and triangular shield; the latter evolved from the previous kite shield. (*Photo and copyright by De Gueules et d'Argent*)

Norman knight wearing a padded *aketon* under his hauberk of chainmail. (*Photo and copyright by Historia Aquitanorum*)

men landed on the Ile de la Cité on Easter Sunday. The Scandinavians plundered Paris with great violence, killing many civilians. After several days, having obtained everything they wanted, they decided to leave the French city, a plague having broken out inside their camp (at that time, the banks of the Seine were covered by marshes, characterized by an inhospitable natural environment). Before returning home, however, the Scandinavians obliged Charles the Bald to pay them an immense sum of money: 7,000 French pounds of gold and silver. This was the first danegeld, or Danish tax, paid by the Frankish monarchs to the Vikings, but was followed by several others. In the 840s, the Scandinavians attacked and pillaged several locations in Normandy, including Rouen, with a predilection for the richest religious sites. Thanks to the presence of many navigable rivers, the Vikings could easily move across northern and central France. Indeed, the Franks were surprised by their capability to sail up-river, and could do very little to effectively oppose the enemy attacks. By penetrating deeply into the very heart of France, the Vikings understood that parts of the country could easily be conquered by them. The Vikings eventually started to attack the interior areas of the Western Franks with more frequency and with larger numbers of warships. The Frankish military system, based on elite field armies that were too large to be rapidly moved, lacked the flexibility to create highly mobile task forces that could counter the raids taking place along the rivers.

In 864, Charles the Bald tried to resolve this problem by issuing the Edict of Pistres, which contained a series of practical measures aimed at protecting French cities and rural areas from the attacks of the Vikings. With the new edict, the Frankish monarch created a large force of cavalry that served on a permanent basis as a special anti-raider corps. All French subjects who were able-bodied and owned a horse had to enlist in the new cavalry force and could be called to serve at very short notice by the royal authorities. The high mobility of cavalry was to counter the rapidity of the Scandinavian raids and enable the French to attack them before they could re-embark on their warships to leave France. The Edict of Pistres also contained other important measures, including an order to build fortified bridges at all the towns located on rivers to prevent the Vikings from sailing into the interior of France as well as from transporting large booties on their ships after their incursions. Unfortunately for the French, however, most of the local communities did not have the necessary resources to build new fortified bridges, and only a few were constructed. The edict promulgated by Charles the Bald also prohibited all trade in weapons with the Scandinavians and the selling of horses to them, with any infraction of the new measures punished by death. Charles the Bald's main objective was to prevent the Scandinavians from establishing permanent bases in his realm. Following the Edict of Pistres, many French nobles started to build castles and fortifications on their lands in order to defend their peasant communities from the constant threat of Viking invasion. The building of private castles reduced the power of the central government and its control over the many nobles of the Kingdom of France, who thereafter became increasingly autonomous, ruling as local monarchs.

During their incursions against Normandy, the Vikings realized that the nearby region of Brittany resented Frankish rule, and so were able to conclude an important

12   Armies of the Normans, 911–1194

Norman knight armed with a mace; note the practice of wearing chainmail only on the leg that was not protected by the shield. (*Photo and copyright by De Gueules et d'Argent*)

Norman knight with nasal helmet and kite shield. (*Photo and copyright by Historia Aquitanorum*)

military alliance with the Bretons. The latter were of Celtic descent and had been subjugated by the Franks only during the reign of Charlemagne. They had strong cultural links with the Britons of Wales and had always tried to preserve their autonomy as much as possible. To oppose the Viking colonization of Normandy and block the initiatives of their Breton alliance, Charles the Bald created a new march (military region) on the eastern borders of Normandy that was called Neustria. This was garrisoned by significant forces and was under the control of Robert the Strong, one of the most experienced Frankish warlords. In 866, a joint Viking/Breton force launched a massive incursion into the territory of Neustria, raiding the important areas of Anjou and Maine. Robert responded by mobilizing his troops and asking for the help of other leading French nobles, notably Rainulf I, Duke of Aquitaine. The Frankish military forces, mostly consisting of cavalry, succeeded in intercepting the Viking/Breton raiders before they could re-embark on their warships and go back to their bases by sailing along through the River Loire. A violent pitched battle soon followed, which resulted in a massacre of the Frankish forces with severe losses. Both Robert the Strong and Rainulf of Aquitaine were killed. In 867, after such a severe defeat, Charles the Bald had no choice but to come to terms with his enemies: he recognized the leader of the Bretons as King of Brittany and ceded the Cotentin peninsula to him. Despite this, the Vikings continued to ravage the valley of the Loire during the following years, with Bourges, Orléans and Angers all sacked. After their previous success, the Vikings launched another three minor incursions against Paris during the 860s, in response to which Charles the Bald promulgated the Edict of Pistres mentioned above. The edict was applied efficiently in the Ile de la Cité, where two new fortified bridges were built on each side of the island to stop the Viking longships. Paris was heavily fortified during the 870s, in view of future Scandinavian attacks. Meanwhile, large-scale Viking raids continued. In 880 and 881, the Scandinavian warriors suffered minor setbacks at the Battle of Thimeon (north of the River Sambre) and Battle of Saucourt-en-Vimeu (near Abbeville), but these did not change the general situation in favour of the Franks, who were still in the process of reorganizing their forces.

In 885, the Vikings launched their largest attack against France, which resulted in the famous siege of Paris. This time, 300 warships with 12,000 warriors entered the mouth of the Seine, with the objective of creating a permanent settlement in northern France. Odo, Count of Paris, was well prepared to receive the invaders, with the city's two new low-lying foot bridges (one made of wood and the other of stone) blocked the passage of the Viking ships. Before their arrival, he built a tower at the head of each bridge to protect them from attacks coming from the banks of the Seine. After reaching Paris, the Vikings demanded the payment of a large sum of money in return for saving the city, but Odo refused to come to terms and siege operations then began. The Scandinavians first attacked the north-eastern tower, which protected the bridge made of wood. They were repulsed with heavy losses by the French defenders, who employed a deadly mixture of hot wax and pitch to stop them. During the following days, the Vikings bombarded the city with siege engines and tried to destroy the bridge with fire, but all attempts failed due to the sturdy resistance of the defenders. The Vikings maintained the siege for two months, building trenches and raiding the nearby countryside in search of supplies. In January 886, they tried to fill the river shallows with debris and plant matter in order to get around the besieged tower, but in the end they decided to change strategy and sent three burning warships against the wooden bridge in an attempt to destroy it. The impact of the burning warships caused serious damage to the bridge, which collapsed a few days later when heavy rain caused a flood of the debris-filled river. The north-eastern tower was by now completely isolated: its remaining twelve defenders refused to surrender and were all killed by the Vikings. At this point, the attackers divided their forces into two, one part remaining on the eastern bank of the Seine in front of Paris while the other sailed up-river to carry out extensive pillaging. Le Mans, Chartres and Evreux were all attacked by the Vikings, who entered the course of the River Loire in order to sack more urban centres.

In May 886, disease began to spread among the ranks of Paris' defenders. The situation became desperate for the Franks, and Odo had no choice but to abandon the city in search of reinforcements. He was later able to return to Paris at the head of a French royal army and to enter the city over the bridge made of stone. By that time, many of the besiegers had already decided to return home and the leadership of those who had remained around Paris was now in the hands of a warlord named Rollo. After another failed attack against the Ile de la Cité and the arrival of substantial Frankish reinforcements, Rollo finally accepted a payment of 700 pounds of silver in exchange for leaving Paris. Odo, as reward for saving the city, became King of France in 888. Paris was safe, but the Viking raids in France continued during the following decades. They were mostly directed against Normandy, where the Scandinavians were finally able to create some permanent settlements around their naval bases, under the guidance of Rollo. Between 810 and 884, the Scandinavians attacked the coastline of present-day Belgium and the Netherlands on several occasions, plundering many settlements and establishing a number of permanent bases. These regions were formally part of West Francia from a political point of view, but they were abandoned to their destiny as the Franks did not have a fleet that could defend them from Viking incursions. Frisia, the northern portion of the Netherlands, was particularly exposed since it bordered the southern part of Denmark and thus could also be attacked by the

Norman knight armed with sword and mace. (*Photo and copyright by Milites Pagenses*)

Norman knight. The early heraldic designs painted on kite shields, like the one shown here, were quite simple. (*Photo and copyright by Historia Aquitanorum*)

Norman heavy infantryman (left) and knight (right). (*Photo and copyright by Historia Aquitanorum*)

Norman knight bearing the standard of his overlord. (*Photo and copyright by Sussex Medieval Society*)

Vikings on land. The Frisians, however, were one of the few Germanic communities of the Frankish Empire who knew how to build effective warships and had good seafaring capabilities, allowing them to organize strong resistance against the raiders. An extensive system of dikes and seawalls was built in order to protect the coastline from Scandinavian landings. Despite all their efforts, however, the Frisians could not prevent the Vikings from establishing some bases on their territory. In 850, Lothair I had no choice but to acknowledge Viking warlord Rorik of Dorestad as his vassal and as the ruler of a large part of Frisia. During 879, a large Viking force, commanded by the Danish leader Godfrid, established a base at Ghent and rapidly assumed control over the whole of Frisia. In 884, at the Battle of Norditi, the Frisians decisively defeated the Scandinavian invaders, who were surprised by the incoming tide during the retreat that followed the clash and suffered heavy losses. Thereafter, the Vikings ceased to be a menace for the Frisians, who started to have a higher degree of political autonomy within the Holy Roman Empire.

In 911, in an attempt to regularize the Viking presence inside the boundaries of his realm, the King of France, Charles the Simple, signed the Treaty of Saint-Clair-sur-Epte with them. Under the terms of the treaty, Rollo was given substantial portions of Norman territory for his men in exchange for his formal submission to the Kingdom of France. The Vikings had to promise that they would defend Normandy from attacks by other Scandinavians, and also had to convert to Christianity. Rollo thus accepted to become a vassal of Charles the Simple in exchange for possession of a vast territory in northern France. In 933, the Scandinavians of Normandy extended their domain by annexing the Cotentin Peninsula of Brittany, which had been colonized by other groups of Norwegian Vikings. Within a few generations, the Vikings living in Normandy had intermarried with the natives and adopted many aspects of their culture. In consequence, around 990, the Viking territories of northern France were officially organized as the Duchy of Normandy and started to be run according to a proper feudal system. While these events took place in northern France, where some form of centralized state existed since the signing of the Treaty of Verdun in 843, the Vikings also pillaged many settlements in southern France, where the Duchy of Aquitaine was ravaged by internal conflict. Employed by the local aristocrats as mercenaries, the Vikings were able to establish a base at the mouth of the River Garonne, from which they launched many incursions into the very heart of France.

Chapter 2

The Duchy of Normandy

The Duchy of Normandy had been officially established in 911, when Charles the Simple and the Viking leader, Rollo, signed the Treaty of Saint-Clair-sur-Epte. The Scandinavians who were already settled in Normandy thereafter became vassals of the French monarch in exchange for being permitted to create their own semi-autonomous country in northern France. The Vikings were given all Norman lands located between the River Epte and the sea, plus Brittany, which had never been under the firm control of the French king so – at least temporarily – the rulers of France decided not to exert their authority over it. In exchange for receiving a new homeland for his followers, Rollo guaranteed his loyalty to Charles the Simple and promised that his warriors would protect the French territories from other Viking groups. The treaty also contained other conditions that the Vikings had to respect: as well as adopting the Christian faith as their new religion, they were to respect the central authority of the French monarchs in various specific administrative fields. Considering that feudalism was developing in France during these years, the compromise between Rollo and Charles the Simple can be seen as a feudal contract between two parties that had very little respect for each other. To seal the treaty, Rollo agreed to be baptized and married Gisela, a legitimate daughter of Charles the Simple. An increasing number of Scandinavians started to settle in the Duchy of Normandy; these, initially called Northmen by the French, soon started to be known as Normans. The early years of Viking presence in Normandy were not easy, the Normans having to abandon paganism and learn to speak French. The fusion between their culture and that of France, however, soon started to have positive results, with many Scandinavian warriors, for example, marrying French women and new Norman families thereby being created. The former Vikings generally had positive relations with the French living both inside and outside the borders of their new territory, but on several occasions they had to fight against the Bretons, who did not accept that their country had been assigned to their former allies. Being the most warlike vassals of the French monarchy, Rollo and his warlords soon started to expand their territorial possessions by moving westward from the valley of the Seine.

In 927, Rollo, who was later considered the first Duke of Normandy, was succeeded by his son, William Longsword, who supported the Gallicizing of his followers and

Norman knight wearing hauberk of chainmail over padded *aketon*. (*Photo and copyright by Milites Pagenses*)

Norman knight standing guard. (*Photo and copyright by Sussex Medieval Society*)

had a positive opinion of contemporary French institutions. For these reasons, soon after assuming power, William had to face a rebellion by some of his warlords who wanted to preserve the Viking identity of their community. The son of Rollo, however, crushed the revolt and later demonstrated himself a capable ruler. Taking advantage of the ongoing internal conflicts that ravaged the Kingdom of France, he convinced the central government to assign him other lands that became part of the Duchy of Normandy: Avranches and the Cotentin Peninsula (which had previously been part of Brittany), as well as the Channel Islands. The Bretons, however, continued to fight to preserve their independence and mounted a strong resistance. William and his Normans, thanks to their military superiority, won a series of clashes against the Bretons, razing to the ground most of their fortifications. Thanks to William Longsword's campaigns, Brittany effectively came under Norman control (albeit only for a short period). During the last years of William's rule, the Normans were heavily involved in the civil wars in France between the various feudal lords, which usually determined the ascendancy of new monarchs. William's fiercest enemy was Arnulf of Flanders, who attacked the Duchy of Normandy and formed an alliance with the Bretons, who were able to reconquer – at least temporarily – several of their territories that had been conquered by the Normans. William Longsword was killed in an ambush – probably organized by Arnulf – in 942.

William was succeeded by his son, Richard, who later became known as Richard I. The new Norman ruler was just a boy and soon came under the control of his father's enemies: Louis IV of France and Arnulf of Flanders. They wanted to wipe out the Normans in northern France, considering them extremely dangerous to the political stability of France. For most of the French aristocrats, the Normans were still viewed as foreigners who had been permitted to settle in France due to the weakness of their central government. The young Richard was taken away from Normandy and placed in the custody of the Count of Ponthieu. Meanwhile, Louis IV tried to divide the Duchy of Normandy in two and to assign them to some of his most trusted allies. The French king, however, was too weak militarily to achieve his ambitious objective of reconquering Normandy. The Normans rebelled against him and obtained the release of their young legitimate ruler. In 946, Richard formed an alliance with the Vikings that were active in other areas of France and went to war against Louis. The French monarch was defeated and captured by the Normans, being released only after having formally recognized Richard as the legitimate Duke of Normandy. Soon after these events, Richard formed an alliance with the main enemy of Louis IV, Hugh, the Count of Paris. Hugh had eyes on the crown of France, for which he needed the support of the Normans. In 947, Richard and Hugh were attacked by King Louis and Arnulf of Flanders, who had been joined by Holy Roman Emperor

Otto I in their anti-Norman efforts. Against all odds, Richard and Hugh prevailed. Their victory led to a long period of peace and stability for the Duchy of Normandy, during which Richard transformed his lands into the most cohesive and powerful of France's feudal principalities. In 955, the son of Hugh of Paris, Hugh Capet, became the new ruler of France. Richard married Emma, a sister of the new king, thereby cementing the alliance between his duchy and the new Capetian royal family. Under Richard I – who was also known as Richard the Fearless because of his courage – the Gallicizing of the Normans was practically complete, the Church also becoming increasingly powerful in Normandy thanks to the construction of several flourishing monasteries.

In 996, Richard II, son of Richard I, became the ruler of Normandy. The new duke was less warlike than his predecessor, but established a solid alliance with both Robert II of France and Geoffrey I of Brittany. Richard II provided the Vikings who raided England with sanctuary and permitted them to sell their plunder in Normandy, acts that clearly violated a treaty that had been signed some years before between Richard I and the Saxon King of England, Aethelred the Unready. The English king mounted an expedition against Normandy with the objective of capturing Richard II, but this ended in complete failure when the Saxon troops disembarking on the Cotentin Peninsula were soundly defeated by the Norman cavalry. By that time, the Normans had adopted the standard military equipment and tactics based on heavy cavalry that were commonly employed in feudal France. Thereafter, Richard tried to establish positive relations with the Kingdom of England, organizing the marriage of his sister Emma to Aethelred. In 1013, Richard II concluded an important alliance with Sweyn Forkbeard, King of Denmark and father of Cnut the Great; when the latter became King of England after Aethelred's death, Richard's sister, Emma, married Cnut. Emma's children included the future King of England, Edward the Confessor, and the future King of Denmark, Harthacnut. In 1026, Richard II died and was succeeded by his eldest son, Richard III, as Duke of Normandy. The reign of Richard III, however, was extremely brief, as immediately after his ascendancy he had to face the rebellion of his younger brother, Robert. While Richard was able to crush the revolt, he died suddenly soon after having defeated his brother. It is highly probable that he was poisoned. Robert duly became the new Duke of Normandy in 1027. He had to pacify his lands after a period of internal unrest, to do which he had to replace several Norman nobles who were still loyal to his brother with men who were supportive of his cause. Many of the aristocrats who were deprived of their lands in Normandy decided to leave France and travelled to southern Italy in search of fortune and a new homeland.

Norman knight from the late twelfth century. (*Photo and copyright by Les Guerriers du Moyen-Age*)

Norman knight from the late twelfth century, wearing great helmet. (*Photo and copyright by Sussex Medieval Society*)

Robert did not have very positive relations with the most important representatives of the Church established in his duchy, confiscating many properties belonging to the clergy. This resulted in the temporary excommunication of Robert, which did not help his pacification of Normandy. The new duke played a prominent role in the feudal wars that ravaged the Kingdom of France, taking advantage of the weakness of the Capetian monarchy. He obtained the region of Vexin from the central government and mounted a major military campaign against Brittany. At that time, the Bretons were ruled by the energetic Alan III, who had expansionist ambitions of his own. Robert later decided to go on a pilgrimage to Jerusalem, probably with the intention of improving his relations with the Church. Before leaving Normandy, he made his only son, the illegitimate William, his heir. In July 1035, while on his pilgrimage, Robert fell ill and died. The ensuing succession was an extremely complex one, since William – known to his enemies as William the Bastard – was just 8 years old. Until 1047, the Duchy of Normandy existed in a state of anarchy, many of the most prominent local nobles having no intention of recognizing William as their legitimate ruler. The young duke was given several different guardians, each of whom tried to pursue their own personal interests. In 1046, the enemies of William mounted a major rebellion and attempted to capture him, but he fled to the Capetian court and organized the reconquest of his duchy with the decisive support of King Henry I of France and the Church. In early 1047, William and Henry won a decisive battle against the rebels near Caen, after which William assumed effective power in Normandy and enacted a Truce of God with the objective of ending the feudal rivalries that had ravaged his duchy for so many years. William soon proved himself a very capable administrator: he travelled constantly around his duchy, confirming charters and collecting revenues, in order to avoid the outbreak of new feudal uprisings and to preserve the economic stability of his realm. He organized his ducal household on several autonomous departments, each of which performed a specific function. William cultivated his alliance with the Church by participating in councils of the clergy and by making in person the appointment of Normandy's bishops. For example, he appointed his loyal half-brother, Odo, as Bishop of Bayeux around 1050.

Over a number of years, William's political and military power increased greatly, which made Henry I suspicious and led to the formation of an alliance between the French king and those Norman nobles who still opposed William. In 1054, the Duchy of Normandy was invaded from two sides by massive armies, but against all odds, William defeated Henry and his internal enemies. Some minor fighting continued until 1060, but with the failed royal invasion of 1054, William's control over Normandy became absolute. In 1057, the duke repulsed another attack directed against his domains, and in 1058 he invaded the County of Dreux. William, being

Norman knight from the late twelfth century, equipped with triangular shield. (*Photo and copyright by Les Guerriers du Moyen-Age*)

Norman knight from the late twelfth century. In the photo it is possible to see the kind of head protection that was worn under the helmet. (*Photo and copyright by Sussex Medieval Society*)

extremely ambitious, needed strong allies in France, to achieve this he married Matilda of Flanders, the daughter of Count Baldwin V of Flanders. Baldwin was one of France's most powerful aristocrats and a warlord who controlled significant military resources. Edward the Confessor, the childless King of England, had previously had very little contact with his grandson, William of Normandy. However, a crisis broke out in England in 1051 between Edward and the man who had been chosen as his successor on the Saxon throne, Harold Godwinson, who was temporarily exiled from England. As a result of the crisis, Edward chose William to replace Harold as his successor. In 1051, the Duke of Normandy visited England and established a strong relationship with Edward the Confessor. After having already enlarged his domains with the County of Dreux, in 1062 William invaded the County of Maine, and after two years of campaigning annexed it to the Duchy of Normandy. In 1064, the duke also invaded Brittany, with the objective of weakening Breton's ruler. When William completed his campaign in Brittany, most of the local aristocrats had become loyal vassals of Normandy. By 1066, when Edward the Confessor died, William was the most powerful warlord in France and was ready to claim the English throne for himself.

Chapter 3

The Norman Conquest of England

On 5 January 1066, the Saxon King of England, Edward the Confessor, died without direct heirs, causing England's worst dynastical crisis of the central centuries of the Middle Ages. Four different pretenders claimed their right to sit on the English throne. The first was Edgar Aetheling, who was aged just 15 in 1066 and was the grandson of Edmund Ironside, who had been King of England for a few months during 1016. The second was Harold Godwinson, Earl of Wessex, who was Edward the Confessor's brother-in-law but had no blood connection with the dead king. The third was Harald Hardrada, Viking King of Norway since 1046, who also had no blood ties with Edward the Confessor. The final claimant was William, Duke of Normandy since 1035, who was a cousin of the king through Edward's mother, Emma, who was William's great-aunt. Edward the Confessor had promised his throne to both William and Harold during two different phases of his long life, which caused great confusion throughout his realm and beyond. The weakest of the pretenders was Edgar Aetheling, the only one who could not count on an army to support his claims. Harald Hardrada was a true Viking and had strong military backing, but his claims on the English throne were weak from a dynastic point of view. Despite this, he decided to invade England after concluding an alliance with Tostig Godwinson, who revolted against his brother Harold Godwinson after the latter was proclaimed King of England in 1066 by the Saxon aristocracy. Politically, Harald Hardrada's landing on English shores was perceived as just another Viking invasion by the local Saxon population. Nevertheless, the Norwegian warlord had a good chance of victory, since in 1066 England was set to be invaded simultaneously by two armies – a Norman attack from the south was thought highly probable – and thus Harold Godwinson would be obliged to divide his forces in two. The Saxon leader could count on the support of the most prominent nobles of his country, who were opposed to the idea of being ruled by a foreigner like the Norman William or the Norwegian Harald. After Edward the Confessor's death, the Saxon nobles swiftly elected Harold as their king in order to gain some time in view of the anticipated invasion of the country by separate Norman and Viking armies.

After hearing of Harold Godwinson's coronation, William of Normandy started assembling a massive fleet in order to transport his army to England. He could count

Norman knight from the late twelfth century, equipped with great helmet and triangular shield. (*Photo and copyright by Les Guerriers du Moyen-Age*)

Norman knight from the late twelfth century, wearing great helmet. (*Photo and copyright by Les Guerriers du Moyen-Age*)

on the support of the English Church and some nobles, who were against Harold's political plans. The new Saxon king prepared to face the Normans and recruited a large army that comprised a significant number of professional warriors. The Saxons deployed on the Isle of Wight and waited for the arrival of the Normans. However, the Normans were blocked in their ports for seven months due to unfavourable weather, meaning William could not carry on with his planned timetable for the invasion. This delay also caused significant problems for Harold, who had planned to defeat the Normans before facing the second invasion led by Harald Hardrada. The Saxon king knew that the Vikings would need several months to gather a sizeable invasion force, unlike the Normans, who were already assembled and would have been able to attack within a few weeks. The delay of seven months suffered by William meant that the two invasions ended up taking place at exactly the same time. Harold knew that the Normans would have to land in southern England, but had no idea where the Vikings would attack. It was assumed that Harald Hardrada's target would be East Anglia or Northumbria. Indeed, the Norwegian Vikings landed on 8 September at the mouth of the River Tyne, with Northumbria as their first target. Harald Hardrada had counted on the support of Tostig Godwinson, who had revolted against his brother, King Harold, and had already tried to form an alliance with William of Normandy. When William refused his offer, Tostig went to the King of Norway and joined him in his invasion of England. The brother of the Saxon monarch was an important ally for Harald Hardrada, since he had intimate knowledge of the terrain on which the Vikings were to operate and was in contact with several of the most powerful Saxon nobles of northern England. After joining his forces with those of Tostig, Harald sailed along the River Ouse towards York. The city had long been the most important land base of the Vikings in England, meaning its capture would be very important for the Scandinavian invasion force.

King Harold had entrusted the defence of the northern part of his kingdom to the two most powerful warlords of the area: the brothers Edwin, the Earl of Mercia, and Morcar, the Earl of Northumbria. The pair had already mobilized part of their forces in anticipation of the Viking invasion, so were able to move swiftly against Harald in order to prevent the fall of York. On 20 September, not far from the city, they clashed with the Scandinavian invaders at the Battle of Fulford. The Viking force numbered some 10,000 men, with the Saxons in a clear numerical inferiority, fielding just 4,500 warriors (3,000 from Northumbria and 1,500 from Mercia). Edwin and Morcar, however, deployed their forces in a very good defensive position that had the River Ouse on its right flank and a swampy area known as the Fordland on the left. Harald deployed his forces on higher ground, but could not conduct any encircling manoeuvre against the wings of his enemy. At the beginning of the clash,

Detail of a great helmet worn by a knight from the late twelfth century. (*Photo and copyright by Les Guerriers du Moyen-Age*)

Norman knight from the late twelfth century. Note the complexity of the heraldic designs. (*Photo and copyright by Les Guerriers du Moyen-Age*)

the Saxons made a massive mistake, as instead of remaining in their strong defensive positions they launched a frontal attack against the Vikings. The Saxon offensive took place while the Scandinavians were still completing the deployment of their troops, but was a complete failure. Harald soon organized a counter-attack with his best warriors and forced the Saxons to give ground. The decisive moment of the battle came when the Vikings were able to cross the River Ouse on one side and the Fordland on the other in order to attack the Saxons on three sides. Outnumbered and outmanoeuvred, the warriors of Edwin and Morcar had no choice but to flee the battlefield. York was occupied by the Vikings soon after their victory, apparently leaving northern England open to conquest by Harald Hardrada. When news of the defeat at Fulford reached Harold Godwinson, the Saxon monarch was shocked but reacted rapidly, force-marching his royal army 190 miles north from London to York in order to prevent the loss of the northern part of his kingdom. Harold proved he was a great military leader by the fact that within a week of the Battle of Fulford, his forces were already facing Harald Hardrada around York.

The Saxon warriors were very tired when they arrived in the north, having marched day and night for a week. However, they were now more numerous than their opponents. According to modern estimates, the Vikings had lost 1,000 men at Fulford, and thus now fielded some 9,000 warriors. Harold, meanwhile, had 10,000 infantry and 2,000 cavalry. The Scandinavians were totally taken by surprise, finding it hard to imagine that the Saxon royal army could reach York in such a short time. The decisive clash of Harald Hardrada's invasion took place at Stamford Bridge, on the River Derwent, on 25 September. When the battle began, some of the Viking forces were on the western bank of the river while the majority were on the eastern bank, since they had no idea that the Saxons were moving towards their positions. Caught by surprise, the Scandinavians on the eastern bank of the Derwent deployed into a defensive circle formation. Those on the western bank were rapidly massacred by the Saxons, with only a few of them able to escape by crossing the bridge that gave the battle its name. At this point of the clash, Harold faced a serious problem, his troops having no option but to pass through the choke-point of the bridge in order to attack the Vikings. According to contemporary sources, a single giant warrior from the army of Harald Hardrada, armed with a two-handed massive axe, blocked the narrow crossing and repulsed the Saxon warriors alone for some time. He killed forty men before a Saxon warrior floated under the bridge and thrust his spear through its planks, mortally wounding the giant axeman. After pouring onto the eastern bank of the Derwent, the Saxons deployed in a battle line just short of the Viking circle, locked their shields and charged against the defensive formation of the enemy. The ensuing phase of the battle, with harsh hand-to-hand fighting, lasted for hours, the Scandinavians resisting with great determination. Both sides suffered heavy losses and the outcome of the clash remained in the balance. Harald Hardrada fought with immense courage among his elite warriors and resisted for as long as possible. Nevertheless, the defensive formation of the Viking army eventually began to fragment and their initial cohesion was lost. The Saxons were finally able to break the enemy wall of shields at various points and gradually started to surround isolated groups of Scandinavians. When it became clear that his army was being outflanked, Harald Hardrada did not abandon the battlefield but continued to fight at the head of his remaining men, being killed by an enemy arrow before his troops collapsed into a state of complete chaos. During this final phase of the clash, which saw the rout of the entire Viking army, Tostig Godwinson was also killed. When everything had seemed lost for the Vikings, some reinforcements arrived on the battlefield, consisting of warriors whom Harald had left behind in order to guard his warships under the command of his prospective son-in-law, Eystein Orre. These men launched a violent counter-attack against the Saxons, but were easily repulsed by Harold's forces, Eystein being killed during the fighting. After several hours of intense combat, Harald Hardrada's impressive Viking army had been completely wiped out. According to contemporary sources, so many Saxons and Norwegians died at Stamford Bridge that the battlefield was still whitened with bleached bones some fifty years later. After obtaining such a brilliant victory, King Harold concluded a truce with the surviving Vikings, who were allowed to leave England after giving pledges not to attack the Saxon kingdom again. The Scandinavian losses were so severe that just twenty-four of their warships returned to Norway. Although Harold had destroyed the forces of one of his rivals, the losses to his own army had been substantial.

Just three days after the Battle of Stamford Bridge, on 28 September, William and his Normans finally landed in southern England, at Pevensey Bay in Sussex. Without having time to replenish his losses and reorganize his troops, Harold had to march south rapidly at the head of his exhausted warriors. For the second time in a few days, the Saxon fighters had to cover an immense distance, and when they arrived in the south to intercept the Normans they were very tired but their morale remained high. It is impossible to predict what might have happened if the Saxons had faced the Normans before meeting Harald Hardrada's army, but Harold probably made a serious strategic mistake when he decided to leave the southern part of his kingdom to stop the invasion of Northumbria. The Norwegians would have needed several weeks to reach the Saxon heartlands, and could have been slowed in their advance by local forces.

40 Armies of the Normans, 911–1194

Norman knight accompanied by two heavy infantrymen. (*Photo and copyright by Historia Aquitanorum*)

The Battle of Hastings, fought on 14 October 1066, is one of the most iconic moments in the military history of the British Isles. The clash there between the Saxons of Harold Godwinson and the Normans of William the Conqueror would shape the destiny of England for the centuries to come. The exact numbers and composition of the Norman invasion force are unknown, but thanks to some details that can be found in different primary sources it is possible to provide an approximate order of battle of William's troops. It has thus been estimated that the Norman army totalled some 13,000 men, with about 10,000 infantry and 3,000 cavalry. The foot

Norman heavy infantryman with hauberk of chainmail worn over a padded aketon. (*Photo and copyright by Sussex Medieval Society*)

soldiers were mostly equipped with helmet and chainmail, like the mounted knights (or *milites*), but a certain number of them were missile troops, comprising archers and crossbowmen. Most of the mounted soldiers were professional fighters from northern France, but they also included a number of lightly equipped mounted servants (squires), who assisted the *milites* as auxiliaries. The missile troops, numbering around 3,000 men, would play an important role during the forthcoming clash. The standard equipment of the Norman soldiers was quite heavy, since it comprised a helmet with nasal and a chainmail hauberk, which in most cases was knee-length and long-sleeved. Both cavalrymen and infantrymen, except for the mounted servants and missile troops, carried a shield made of wood and reinforced on the external edges with a strip of metal. The shield was kite-shaped for most of the cavalry and infantry, but some of the latter had round shields similar to those of the Saxons. The main weapon of the Norman knights, in addition to the longsword, was the couched lance that was carried tucked against the body under the right arm. The infantry had a longer spear that was used like a pike. Missile troops wore no armour, except for a simple conical helmet. The Saxon army opposing the Normans consisted of 12,000–13,000 soldiers, meaning the sides were equally matched, but had a different internal composition. Harold's forces did not include large contingents of cavalry or missile troops, except for a few archers, meaning the Saxon army that fought at Hastings was largely a compact infantry force. Some 3,000 of the Saxon warriors were elite housecarls (professional fighters in royal service), while the remaining 10,000 were thegns (professionals, but inferior to the housecarls) or fyrdmen (non-professional fighters). The thegns came from several areas of England, having been mobilized by Harold to face the Scandinavian invasion of Harald Hardrada. The fyrdmen, instead, mostly came from the regions of southern England that were exposed to the Norman invasion. Harold, after defeating the Vikings in the north, had left some of his troops in northern England under the orders of Morcar and Edwin in order to prevent any further Norwegian attempt to attack his realm. With the best elements of his army, Harold had marched south rapidly, stopping for just a few days in London. It is likely that the Saxon troops spent about a week on their march south, averaging around 27 miles per day, which was absolutely incredible by the standards of the time. On the night of 13 October, Harold and his men camped on Caldbec Hill and started to prepare for the upcoming battle. The Saxon monarch had no precise information about the composition of William's forces, but wanted to intercept them before they could move further inland. It was the Normans, however, who advanced first.

Harold established a very strong defensive position at the top of Caldbec Hill, deploying his men in a massive shield wall. Behind the ordinary infantrymen were the housecarls (who were to be used as a strategic reserve) and the few missile troops. The position had been chosen well, as launching a frontal attack against the Saxon positions on Caldbec Hill would be extremely difficult for the Normans, who would suffer severe losses during their advance (caused by the missiles thrown by the enemy) and would have to cross a wide extent of broken terrain before reaching the enemy positions. Harold understood all this very well and thus decided to fight a defensive battle, his decision also influenced by the fact that his troops were extremely tired after having marched for many days to reach the battlefield, and consequently in no condition to launch a massive attack. The clash took place at the present-day town of Battle in East Sussex, between Caldbec Hill to the north and Telham Hill to the south. Harold's forces were deployed in a small but dense formation at the top of a steep slope, with their flanks protected by woods and with some marshy ground in front of them. It was a perfect defensive position. William arranged his troops in three groups, or battles, which were assembled according to the geographical provenance of the various soldiers. The left battle consisted of soldiers from Brittany, Anjou, Poitou and Maine, regions that were all under the control of the Duchy of Normandy, the most important of which was Brittany. The central group comprised the best of William's soldiers, hailing from Normandy and commanded by William

Norman heavy infantryman equipped with nasal helmet. (*Photo and copyright by Historia Aquitanorum*)

Norman heavy infantryman. (*Photo and copyright by Historia Aquitanorum*)

himself. The right battle was made up of soldiers from Picardy, Boulogne and Flanders; these included a good number of mercenaries, who were not feudal levies but professional soldiers. The front lines of each battle were made up of archers and a few crossbowmen, with the infantrymen deployed behind the missile troops and the cavalry held in reserve. William wanted to open the battle with his excellent archers, in order to weaken the strong defensive positions of Harold with a rain of arrows. His plan was to order an infantry charge after the attack by his light troops, and these foot soldiers would create openings in the Saxon ranks that could be exploited by a final cavalry charge to decide the outcome of the battle in the Normans' favour.

The Normans attacked first, but from the beginning of the battle it was clear that William's original plan was not going to work, the archers shooting uphill at the Saxon shield wall with very little effect. The angle at which they were firing meant that the arrows either bounced on the Saxon shields or overshot their targets. Having seen that his missile troops were of little use, William ordered an attack by his infantry. The Norman foot soldiers, however, were met with a barrage of missiles (including axes and stones, in addition to arrows) and were unable to open any gap in the enemy shield wall. The cavalry then joined the infantry in the attack, but few of the Norman *milites* were even able to reach the top of the hill, being bogged down by their heavy equipment. At this point of the battle, a rumour started that William

The Norman Conquest of England 45

Norman heavy infantryman bearing spear and kite shield. (*Photo and copyright by Historia Aquitanorum*)

Norman heavy infantryman. (*Photo and copyright by Historia Aquitanorum*)

had been killed; this caused great confusion among the Normans, many of whom started retreating. The Saxons then began attacking the Normans as they fell back, but William rode through his forces, showing his face and shouting that he was still alive. At this point, a Norman counter-attack was organized, which stopped the Saxon offensive and caused a temporary break in the fighting. The Saxon attack repulsed by the Normans was a spontaneous one, having not been ordered by Harold, who had no wish to abandon his strong defensive positions. During the lull in the fighting, which probably occurred in the early afternoon, the opposing sides took the opportunity to rest and have some food. William, meanwhile, came up with a new battle plan, one inspired by the events of the morning. He had worked out that the Saxons would become extremely vulnerable if they abandoned their positions on top of the hill. If they could be tempted to move down onto the plain, the Norman cavalry could charge against the Saxon infantry and cause them severe losses.

When the fighting resumed, William twice sent his cavalry against the Saxons, the Normans attacking for just a few minutes before making a feigned flight in the hope of inducing their enemies to move from the hill and launch a counter-attack. Several Saxon soldiers duly abandoned their positions and followed after the retreating Norman horsemen in close pursuit, but by abandoning the wall of shields that had been deployed by Harold they became an easy target for William's missile troops. Once in the plain, the Saxons were halted by the Norman infantry and then charged by their cavalry, who had turned around from their feigned retreat. Being on the open field and having no time to deploy in a defensive formation, the vulnerable Saxon warriors were massacred by the Norman *milites* in several deadly charges. Harold, unable to keep discipline among the ranks of his army, was killed during this chaotic phase of the battle while he was trying to stop his men. The Saxon king is said in some sources to have died from an arrow to the eye: whatever the case, his sudden death left the Saxon troops leaderless in the most delicate moment of the struggle. Most of the thegns and fyrdmen had abandoned their positions on the top of the hill, and were progressively routed by the Normans on the plain. The housecarls, meanwhile, largely retained their discipline and remained on top of the hill to defend the body of their king. They continued to fight there until the last of them was killed by the now overwhelmingly superior Norman forces. With the death of Harold and his formidable housecarls at Hastings, William of Normandy became 'the Conqueror' and the history of the British Isles changed forever. The history of Norman England had just begun.

Chapter 4

The Reign of William the Conqueror

After crushing the Saxon army at Hastings, William hoped that the conquest of his new realm could be rapidly completed. However, the Saxon nobles and clergy refused to just surrender, instead nominating Edgar Aetheling – son of Edmund Ironside – as their king and organizing further resistance against the Norman invaders. William showed his intelligence with his first moves in England, securing Dover – transforming it into his main naval base from which supplies and reinforcements could come from Normandy – and the important religious centre of Canterbury. He then sent a token force to occupy Winchester, where the Saxon royal treasury was kept. In late November 1066, he entered London without facing any serious opposition. After crossing the River Thames, William seized control of most of southern England, as a result of which, several of the Saxon aristocrats who had decided to resist after Hastings – including Edgar Aetheling – submitted to the Norman ruler without putting up a fight. On Christmas Day, William was crowned King of England at Westminster Abbey. The new monarch, knowing very well that those in northern England would resent his rule, tried to form a solid alliance with those Saxon nobles who had joined his cause by confirming them in their lands and titles. The various bishops were also all confirmed, William being well aware of the great power that the Church had in England. Soon after assuming power in his new kingdom, William went back to Normandy for a few months in order to stabilize his political position in northern France, where one of his former local allies, Eustace of Boulogne, was revolting against him. While the Norman king was absent, the Saxons reorganized themselves in northern and western England under the guidance of Harold Godwinson's mother, Gytha. She had the centre of her power in the city of Exeter, where the Saxon resistance gathered a good portion of its military forces. In December 1067, William returned to England and invested Exeter, which was taken by the Normans after a short siege. Meanwhile, various other relatives of Harold, including his sons, landed near Bristol with the objective of launching a major revolt, but were defeated by local Norman forces.

In 1068, the Saxon warlords Edwin and Morcar, who had temporarily supported William after the Saxon defeat at Hastings, rose up against the Normans. The revolt by two of the most influential Saxon nobles represented a serious problem for King

William, who soon understood that the only way to assume effective control over his entire realm was to defeat the rebels and replace them with loyal Norman nobles. Feudalism, which was well established in Normandy, did not exist at the time in England, so a new nobility made up of landowners had to be created almost from scratch. Additionally, the Normans built a network of castles across England, which strengthened their hold on the realm. These fortifications were assigned to the new English nobles coming from Normandy and were defended by substantial garrisons. The period after the uprising of Edwin and Morcar was characterized by a series of devastating military campaigns conducted in northern England, the Normans employing very harsh repressive methods in order to end all Saxon resistance. This 'Harrying of the North' was one of the most controversial moves made by King William. In the summer of 1068, he invaded Northumbria and occupied York, but soon after the main Norman army left the city the garrison left behind by the king was besieged by Saxon forces. William had to swiftly return to Northumbria and defeat the local rebels again. Meanwhile, further minor Saxon uprisings broke out in practically every corner of his kingdom. By now, Edgar Aetheling had also changed sides and launched a campaign against Norman rule. Edgar realized that without help from abroad, he would never be able to defeat the invaders, so he made an alliance with Sweyn II, who was King of Denmark and a nephew of Cnut the Great.

Sweyn assembled a large fleet commanded by his sons and sent it to the coast of Northumbria. The Danes raided the eastern coastline of England before capturing York and joining forces with the Saxon insurgents. This new menace was a particularly serious one for King William, as the Scandinavian warriors who were now on English soil were professional fighters. In the winter of 1069, William marched with his royal army from Nottingham to York in a bid to defeat the Danes in battle, but when he reached the city he found that the raiders had already moved with all their ships to the Humber Estuary. Negotiations then took place between William and the Danish leaders, after which the king agreed to pay a large sum of money to the Scandinavians in exchange for their promise to leave England immediately without further fighting. After the Danish menace disappeared, William turned his attention back to the Saxon rebels. He and his men acted in a very cruel way: many villages were burned to the ground, crops and herds were confiscated, hundreds of civilians were killed without reason and local communities' reserves of food were destroyed. These acts caused the death of over 100,000 people, mostly from starvation. William's devastating psychological warfare to terrorize his enemies and eradicate forever any form of Saxon resistance in northern England was accompanied by the building of many new castles, most of which were initially only small fortifications made of wood rather than massive stone constructions. One by one, all the rebel Saxon aristocrats

Norman heavy infantryman wearing a decorated version of nasal helmet. (*Photo and copyright by Milites Pagenses*)

Norman heavy infantryman. (*Photo and copyright by Milites Pagenses*)

Norman heavy infantryman with hauberk of chainmail worn over a padded *aketon*. (*Photo and copyright by Historia Aquitanorum*)

Norman heavy infantryman armed with axe. (*Photo and copyright by Les Guerriers du Moyen-Age*)

surrendered, with new Norman castles built in various areas of the country: from Chester, Lincoln, Nottingham and York to Cambridge, Huntingdon, Stafford and Warwick. By April 1070, William had completely pacified the northern part of his kingdom, and could turn his attention to creating a strong alliance with the English clergy. His conquest of the realm was officially recognized by the Pope, who sent three of his legates to Winchester to crown William again. In exchange for this symbolically important religious investiture, the Norman monarch agreed to replace several Saxon bishops and abbots with new French ones who could be controlled more easily by the Pope.

However, King William still had to face various menaces coming from abroad to the stability of his kingdom. In the spring of 1070, Sweyn of Denmark attacked England again at the head of a large fleet. The Danish king joined forces with local Saxon insurgents, but after several weeks of campaigning he was able to achieve very little – except for looting some religious buildings – and thus returned home. During 1071, William fought once again against his main Saxon enemies, Edwin and Morcar. Edwin was betrayed by his own men and killed, but Morcar went to the Isle of Ely in East Anglia where he continued his resistance. The Normans responded by attacking Ely, and defeating and capturing Morcar. In 1072, William had to face a new foreign invasion, this time coming from the north, King Malcolm of Scotland invading northern England in the hope of gaining some border territories thanks to the internal troubles experienced by the Normans. William easily defeated Malcolm after a brief campaign and concluded a peace treaty with him; according to this, Edgar Aetheling, who had sought refuge in Malcolm's court, was expelled from Scotland. During 1073, William again had to leave England for Normandy when his continental possession of Maine was attacked by the Count of Anjou. After several weeks of fighting, the Norman king was able to prevail, but the general strategic situation of his French domains was worsening. The Counts of Anjou and Flanders were determined to limit Norman power in northern France. To achieve this, they received the potentially decisive support of the King of France, who feared that William could become more powerful than himself. In 1075, two of the leading Norman nobles who had received land properties in England – Ralph de Gael, the Earl of Norfolk, and Roger de Breteuil, the Earl of Hereford – organized a plot to overthrow William known as the 'Revolt of the Earls', which was sponsored and supported by the King of France. Although William was absent when the rebellion broke out, his loyal vassals were swiftly able to crush the revolt alone. The insurgents had invited a Danish fleet of 200 warships to England, but this arrived too late to influence events.

Soon after, William had to face an invasion of his Norman domains by King Philip I of France, who by 1076 was determined to reduce the territorial extent and political power of the Duchy of Normandy. During this new conflict, for the first time in his long military career, William the Conqueror was defeated on the open field at the Battle of Dol. Despite this temporary setback, however, the Normans defeated enemy forces that later tried to invade Maine. During 1077, hostilities between William and Philip temporarily came to an end, but the King of England started to experience serious troubles within his family. Robert, the eldest son of William, quarrelled with his younger brothers William and Henry in view of the succession to their father. The ruling Duke of Normandy was now also King of England, but would his successor continue to control both territories or would they be divided? Would Robert be given Normandy or England? In 1078, Robert, who wanted to receive Normandy before the death of his father, rebelled against William. He received strong support from Philip of France, who assigned him the castle of Gerberoi on the border of Normandy. King William besieged his son and the rebels in Gerberoi. There was also a pitched battle between the opposing sides, during which William was unhorsed by Robert. The king was saved by one of his English soldiers, but the battle was lost and he had to abandon the siege. In 1080, father and eldest son finally found a compromise, according to which the Duchy of Normandy was promised to Robert, a reward he desired more than the English crown; Normandy, after all, was richer than England at that time, and many Norman nobles still considered William's conquest of England only as a temporary addition to Norman domains. While King William was campaigning in Normandy against Robert, King Malcolm of Scotland invaded northern England in the area between the rivers Tweed and Tees. Encouraged by the attack, the local Northumbrians rebelled against the Normans. William responded by sending his son Robert against the Scots at the head of an army. Malcolm and the Northumbrian rebels were defeated, and the Normans built new fortifications to defend the border with Scotland. During 1083, Robert rebelled again against his father and renewed his alliance with the King of France; as a result, William went back to Normandy to fight in Maine to crush a feudal revolt. The last years of William's long reign were troubled ones, with him having to fight against the French monarch in Vexin. In July 1087, while burning the city of Mantes in Vexin, King William suffered a fatal injury, probably caused by the pommel of his saddle. Before dying, William the Conqueror assigned the Duchy of Normandy to his first son, Robert, and gave custody of the Kingdom of England to his second son, William. Henry, his younger son, did not inherit any territories, but did receive a large sum of money. William, soon after the death of his father, was crowned King of England as William II.

Norman heavy infantryman armed with Danish axe and mace. (*Photo and copyright by Sussex Medieval Society*)

The Reign of William the Conqueror 57

Norman heavy infantryman from the Kingdom of Sicily. He is wearing a corselet of scale armour over his hauberk. (*Photo and copyright by Les Guerriers du Moyen-Age*)

William the Conqueror was a capable military leader but also an excellent administrator. He created an impressive network of fortifications in England, comprising castles but also keeps and mottes. The Tower of London was also erected during his reign. William introduced feudalism in his new realm, assigning land properties to his most loyal nobles who – in turn – gave fiefdoms to the knights at their service (the sub-infeudation system). Each of the Norman earls was to provide a fixed quota of knights to the king, not only for war service but also as garrisons for the various castles in peacetime. William was well known for his love of hunting and introduced the 'forest law' in several areas of England, according to which only authorized individuals could hunt in the royal forests. He never attempted to integrate Normandy and England into one unified political entity, meaning that through his French domains he remained a vassal of the French monarchy. William did not reform the Saxon administrative system based on shires, meaning royal authority continued to be represented in each of these areas by public officials known as sheriffs. The king spent most of his reign travelling across his domains in order to ensure Norman control of the various territories. Initially, he had very little knowledge of his new subjects' economic capabilities or his new realm's resources. William, however, continued the collection of the Saxon danegeld, an annual land tax based on the value of landholdings, which could be collected at differing rates (usually two shillings per hide in normal years, increasing to six shillings in times of crisis). William enlarged the royal possessions in England by absorbing the lands previously owned by Harold Godwinson, which made him the largest secular landowner in the kingdom by a wide margin. At Christmas 1085, William ordered the compilation of a survey of the landholdings held by himself and his vassals throughout England, and also decided to divide his realm into counties. This resulted in the survey known as the Domesday Book, a listing made on a county basis that gave the holdings of each landholder grouped by owners. The document described each holding in great detail, providing its value and tax assessment as well as other information (such as the number of peasants living on it, the number of ploughs that the locals had and the location of any significant natural or material resource). The Domesday Book, which was completed during 1086, is the most impressive record of feudal obligations ever produced during the Middle Ages, a perfect representation of William the Conqueror's great administrative ability.

Chapter 5

Norman England Under William II and Henry I

King William II, also known as William Rufus or William the Red because of the colour of his hair, faced a series of political problems soon after becoming the King of England. Many Norman nobles held land properties on both sides of the Channel and had always been vassals of a single overlord, William the Conqueror. Following his death, these aristocrats became vassals of William II for their English possessions and of Duke Robert – nicknamed Robert Curthose or Robert Short Stockings by his father – for their French possessions. Being vassals of two lords who were probably going to fight each other in the near future was not easy to sustain in the long run, and many Norman nobles were in favour of reuniting England and Normandy under a single monarch. Robert was considered more expert and ambitious than his younger brother, and several of the most powerful Norman lords living in England organized a revolt against their new king in 1088. This rebellion was led by Bishop Odo of Bayeux, half-brother of William the Conqueror, who had been deprived of much of his personal power during the latter's later reign. The rebel nobles planned their insurrection effectively, taking control of key castles and stocking large amounts of provisions. However, William II's response to their actions was both rapid and effective. As a first move, the young king promised those warlords who decided to fight on his side that they would receive as much money and land as they wanted. He then tried to win the favour of the English commoners by promising that he would promulgate new and fairer laws. Both moves worked well: several aristocrats who had initially joined the revolt changed their mind and remained loyal to the legitimate king, while most of the common people started to consider William as someone who could improve their living conditions. King William's forces, thanks to their numerical superiority, were able to crush the rebellion quite rapidly. Odo was besieged in Pevensey Castle and captured when the stronghold fell. Robert Curthose, uncertain about the outcome of events, never left Normandy for England, and the troops he had assembled to join Odo did not arrive in time. At the end of hostilities, William II was officially recognized as the legitimate King of England by his brother Robert.

In 1091, hostilities resumed between William II and Robert, with the king attempting to invade the Duchy of Normandy. This conflict, however, was short-lived,

Norman heavy infantryman wearing *chapel de fer* helmet. (*Photo and copyright by Les Guerriers du Moyen-Age*)

ending without any significant modification to the status quo. William II, in fact, had to abandon his campaign in France when northern England came under attack from Malcolm III of Scotland. The invasion by the Scots was repulsed, after which Carlisle Castle was built by the Normans to strengthen control over Cumberland and Westmorland, the areas claimed by Malcolm III. In 1093, the Scottish king invaded England again, ravaging Northumbria for some time, until he was killed together with his son and heir at the Battle of Alnwick on 13 November. The throne of Scotland was then seized by Malcolm's brother, Donald, but William did not

Norman heavy infantryman wearing a taller version of the *chapel de fer* helmet. (*Photo and copyright by Les Guerriers du Moyen-Age*)

recognize his ascendancy. The main objective of the English monarch was now to weaken the Scots by provoking a civil war between two opposing pretenders; he first supported the claims of Malcolm's son, Duncan, and then of another of Malcolm's sons, named Edgar. Between 1094 and 1097, Edgar fought against his uncle Donald with the support of the Normans, and was finally able to obtain the throne of his father. After becoming absolute ruler of Scotland, Edgar ceded Lothian to King William and attended his court. William II was thus the first English monarch who played a significant role in the internal politics of Scotland and tried to extend his influence north of Northumbria. William was also the first King of England to campaign in Wales, which was still fully independent from England, meaning he had to secure control over the border dividing his lands from those of the Welsh. He conducted two forays into Wales during 1097 and built a series of castles along the border, the backbone of the future Marcher Lordships, border fiefdoms assigned to the most warlike Norman nobles.

In 1096, Robert Curthose, who had been suffering in terms of prestige from his younger brother's successes, decided to join the First Crusade (see Chapter 7). To fund his venture, he mortgaged the Duchy of Normandy to William II in return for the payment of 10,000 marks. The King of England took the opportunity represented by his brother's unexpected offer and levied a special tax in his realm in order to pay the sum requested by Robert. Consequently, when Robert left Europe for the Holy Land, William II started to rule Normandy as regent. The King of England strove to protect the borders of the duchy from the expansionist ambitions of the French monarchy, twice campaigning on the continent (in 1097 and 1099), and obtaining some positive results. William secured Maine but failed to reconquer that part of the Vexin region that had been lost by the Normans during the later years of his father's reign. William II, like his father, was an excellent administrator and a skilled politician. Regarding relations with the Church, he was able to retain full control over the national clergy without coming into direct conflict with the papacy. At that time, the Gregorian Reform of the Church was trying to transform the Pope into a universal monarch, exerting his power over all the Christian realms of Europe. William II preserved the autonomy of his clergy but always had positive relations with the papacy. On 2 August 1100, while hunting near Brockenhurst, William II was accidentally shot by an arrow and killed. The sudden death of the king took both his brothers by surprise. When William died, Robert Curthose was returning from the First Crusade and was already raising funds to buy back his Duchy of Normandy. However, Robert did not reach Normandy in time, as soon after his father's death, his younger brother, Henry, hastened to Winchester where he secured possession of the royal treasury and then moved rapidly to London, where he was crowned King of England on 5 August.

Upon his return to Normandy, Robert, supported by several Norman nobles who believed that William II's death was the result of a plot orchestrated by Henry, claimed the English throne for himself and started to prepare an invasion of England. Henry, who had been crowned as Henry I, worked to secure his control over England before his brother landed in the country. He announced that he would abandon William II's rigid policies towards the Church, promised to prevent royal abuses of the feudal lords' property rights and proclaimed that he would initiate a new age of peace for his realm. He gave lands and money to the major Norman aristocrats of England and – to secure his northern borders – married Matilda, daughter of Malcolm III of Scotland. By July 1101, Robert was ready to invade England with his army, while Henry was still experiencing serious military difficulties. Several of his most powerful warlords decided not to join the royal army but to await the development of events. Only the contingents raised from the ecclesiastical land properties attended the military camp built by the king, where they underwent training for the upcoming campaign. Robert Curthose landed at Portsmouth on 20 July at the head of an army that was

Norman sergeant from the late twelfth century, wearing iron greaves. (*Photo and copyright by Les Guerriers du Moyen-Age*)

Norman sergeant from the late twelfth century, armed with falchion. (*Photo and copyright by Les Guerriers du Moyen-Age*)

quite small but well equipped, and was soon joined by several Norman aristocrats who supported his cause. Robert, instead of marching on Winchester to seize the royal treasure, made the great mistake of waiting for the arrival of more troops loyal to him. This enabled Henry to assemble his forces and move towards him. They met in Alton, Hampshire, but instead of fighting the two brothers initiated peace negotiations. Both were in quite a weak military position and could not be confident about the outcome of any eventual battle. The negotiations led to the signing of the Treaty of Alton, according to which Robert recognized Henry as the legitimate King of England and Henry renounced all his claims on Normandy. Despite the treaty, the King of England inflicted severe penalties on the nobles who had stood against him during the invasion. Henry had only signed the treaty to gain valuable time to secure his political position in England, never abandoning his hopes of seizing the Duchy of Normandy from his brother.

During 1103 and 1104, Henry allied himself with the most powerful aristocrats of Normandy, offering them lands and titles in exchange for their loyalty. He was slowly isolating his brother, who could now count on very few military resources. In 1105, after Robert had been abandoned by most of his previous supporters, Henry sent a token force of knights to Normandy in order to provoke a confrontation with his brother. When these knights were captured by Robert, Henry launched his invasion of the duchy. However, the 1105 campaign in Normandy was a failure for the king, who captured some important cities but was unable to defeat his brother. In 1106, Henry invaded again, this time at the head of a larger force. In September of that year, the decisive confrontation of the campaign took place at Tincherbray. Robert attacked first with his cavalry, but Henry responded by investing the enemy flanks with his reserves commanded by his French allies (the Count of Maine and the Duke of Brittany). Robert was defeated and taken prisoner. After crushing any form of resistance in Normandy, Henry sent his older brother to Devizes Castle in Wiltshire, where he was imprisoned for two decades before being moved to Cardiff where he died as a captive in 1134 (just a few months before his younger brother). After the events of 1106, the Duchy of Normandy and the Kingdom of England were ruled by the same monarch until the Norman dynasty came to an end. The fact that Normandy and England were again under control of a single person caused serious trouble for Henry, as had happened to his father, William the Conqueror, because the new King of France – Louis VI, ruling since 1108 – had plans to assert his power over the most important French feudal lords, including the Duke of Normandy. Louis demanded that Henry pay homage to him like any other vassal of the French crown, but the King of England refused and the situation seemed to be on the verge of causing a new war. After both sides mobilized their forces along the borders of Normandy, the crisis was resolved with peace negotiations, which led to the stipulation of a temporary truce and left the most important issues unresolved. In 1111, taking advantage of a feudal rebellion that was taking place in France against Louis VI, Henry landed in Normandy at the head of an army and joined forces with those of the French nobles who were fighting against the French king. In March 1113, after having suffered several defeats, Louis decided to end hostilities and negotiated a peace settlement with Henry, who received some disputed fortresses on Normandy's borders and was confirmed as the feudal overlord of Maine.

While these events took place on the continent, the situation on the Welsh border of England was deteriorating. In 1108, Henry I had conducted his first major campaign in Wales, which was largely successful and resulted in the Norman colonization of the area around Pembroke. In 1114, however, the newly settled Norman lords were attacked by some of the strongest Welsh leaders. To restore order in the Welsh Marches, Henry had to send three armies into Wales and to ask for the help of his ally King Alexander of Scotland. This campaign was also a success for Henry, but he was unable to decisively defeat the Welsh. The Welsh Marches came back under firm English control – helped by the building of further castles – but no other Welsh lands were seized by Henry. Over time, especially after 1115, the King of England became increasingly concerned about his succession. He in particular wanted to have his son, William Adelin, recognized as the future legitimate Duke of Normandy by Louis VI. However, Louis refused all Henry's offers and continued to affirm that for him the legitimate future Duke of Normandy was William Clito, son of Robert Curthose. In 1116, the existing political issues led to the resumption of hostilities between Henry and Louis. The numerical superiority of the French obliged Henry to adopt a defensive strategy, which resulted in the pillaging of much of the Norman countryside. During 1118, most of the Norman nobles fighting in northern France abandoned Henry and changed sides, but the king continued to resist against his enemies. In 1119, the forces of Henry and Louis clashed at the Battle of Brémule in Vexin. Against all odds, Henry was able to prevail and obtain a great victory. After his success at Brémule, hostilities in France slowly came to an end, with the final signing of a peace treaty. William Adelin was thereby recognized as the future legitimate Duke of Normandy in exchange for accepting to pay homage to Louis VI.

Henry I was proving himself an excellent monarch. He spent most of his rule travelling across his domains, creating an itinerant royal court that was made up of various components: the chapel – headed by the chancellor – that looked after the royal documents; the chamber, that dealt with financial affairs; and the office of the master-marshal, who was responsible for logistical and military matters. The court, or *familia regis*, also included the elite knights of the royal household, which

Norman spearman with padded *aketon*. (*Photo and copyright by De Gueules et d'Argent*)

Norman spearman with kite shield. (*Photo and copyright by Milites Pagenses*)

Norman England Under William II and Henry I   69

Norman spearman with nasal helmet.
(*Photo and copyright by De Gueules et d'Argent*)

were at the king's direct orders and could serve in any corner of his domains. Henry was responsible for the development of the Royal Exchequer, which was created to collect and audit the revenues sent by the sheriffs from the various shires. Eyre or itinerant courts of justice came into being and many new laws were promulgated during Henry's long reign. The monarch also reformed coinage three times and introduced new administrative institutions – similar to the English ones – in Normandy. Soon after it seemed that the peace agreements of 1120 had resolved his succession problems, however, a tragedy struck Henry. His son and successor, William Adelin, died in the sinking of the royal vessel known as the White Ship on 25 November 1120. This unexpected event left Henry with no legitimate son, as a result of which he announced his intention to take a new wife in order to produce a new heir. The death of William Adelin, however, destroyed the balance of power that Henry had created with so much difficulty in northern France. His French enemies encouraged a new rebellion by the Norman aristocrats and attacked the borders of the Duchy of Normandy. During 1123 and 1124, the English king had to send most of his forces to the continent to conduct costly campaigns against his enemies there. Eventually, the feudal revolt in Normandy was crushed. By 1125, the old king had not yet conceived any new children and thus the future of his dynasty appeared at risk.

Henry had a legitimate daughter, Matilda, who had married the ruling

Norman spearman with large triangular shield. (*Photo and copyright by De Gueules et d'Argent*)

Holy Roman Emperor a few years before and now lived in Germany. Having little alternative, and realizing that he would never have another legitimate son, Henry chose Matilda as his heir in 1126, soon after her husband died. England had never been ruled by a queen, and his decision caused great malcontent. During 1127 and 1128, Henry was again involved in campaigning on the continent against Louis VI, who refused to recognize Matilda as the legitimate heir to the Norman possessions. After the death of William Clito, however, hostilities came to an end as the King of France had no other potential heir to support against Matilda. In 1128, Henry organized the marriage of Matilda to Geoffrey of Anjou, one of the most powerful nobles of France. Matilda and Geoffrey made a very ambitious couple. In 1135, they started to urge Henry to hand over the Duchy of Normandy to them while he was still alive, but the old monarch refused to do so. On 1 December of that year, after Matilda and Geoffrey had revolted against him, Henry I died of natural causes. With the death of the last surviving son of William the Conqueror, a new historical phase, known as The Anarchy, began in England and Normandy. Most of the Norman nobles did not recognize Matilda as Henry's legitimate heir, and instead proclaimed Stephen of Blois – son of William's daughter, Adela – the new King of England. During the period from 1135–54, England and Normandy were ravaged by a series of military campaigns between the supporters of Matilda and Stephen. In the end, upon Stephen's death, it was Matilda's son, Henry, who became Duke of Normandy and King of England. He was crowned as Henry II and initiated a new royal family, the Plantagenet dynasty, which was completely different from the previous line in being Angevin (from Geoffrey of Anjou) rather than Norman.

Chapter 6

The Norman Conquest of Southern Italy

Following the fall of the Western Roman Empire, southern Italy had several centuries characterized by foreign invasions and political fragmentation. Occupied by the Ostrogoths like the rest of the Italian peninsula, it was later reconquered by the Eastern Roman Empire during the reign of Justinian. The Eastern Romans, or Byzantines, tried to establish a solid presence in southern Italy, and especially in Sicily, since the island produced large amounts of grain and was located in the centre of the Mediterranean. In 568, however, the warlike Germanic people of the Lombards invaded Italy from Pannonia (modern Hungary), marching down the peninsula devastating most of the rural areas. The Byzantines, being quite weak militarily, could do very little to stop the Lombard penetration into Italy, but did organize a resistance that prevented the Germanic tribesmen from conquering the whole of the peninsula. Large portions of continental southern Italy – in particular those areas located along the coastline – and the whole island of Sicily remained under Byzantine control. On land, the Lombard forces were superior to those of the Byzantines, who usually had very limited numbers of troops in Italy. At sea, however, the Byzantine navy was no opposition from the Lombards, who had no warships and were not a seafaring people. Territories taken by the Lombards in Italy were gradually organized into two main political entities: Langobardia Maior (or Greater Langobardia) and Langobardia Minor (Lesser Langobardia), the first comprising northern Italy and much of central Italy, while the latter a small portion of central Italy and the Lombard possessions in southern Italy. Lesser Langobardia consisted of two autonomous duchies, which were completely independent from the Lombard Kingdom of Greater Langobardia: the Duchy of Spoleto in central Italy and the Duchy of Beneventum in southern Italy. The latter comprised all the interior areas of continental southern Italy, and thus bordered with Byzantine lands. The Duchy of Beneventum and the Byzantines were almost constantly at war with each other, but after the major military campaigns of the Lombard conquest, warfare in southern Italy soon became a matter of guerrilla operations conducted by both the Lombards and Byzantines with hit-and-run tactics. The Lombards were unable to besiege the large Byzantine coastal centres that could be easily supplied from the sea, while the Byzantines were too weak to penetrate into the mountain areas of the

Norman infantryman armed with spear and throwing javelin. (*Photo and copyright by Milites Pagenses*)

Norman infantryman wearing *cervelliere* (hemisphere) helmet and armed with mace. (*Photo and copyright by Les Guerriers du Moyen-Age*)

interior where the Lombards were established. In 773, the Franks of Charlemagne, at the invitation of the Pope, invaded Italy and crushed the armies of the Lombard Kingdom. As a result, the whole of Greater Langobardia was absorbed into the Frankish domains that – a few years later – were reorganized by Charlemagne as the Holy Roman Empire. Soon after the fall of Greater Langobardia, the Duchy of Spoleto in central Italy was also occupied by the Franks, but the Duchy of Beneventum remained independent thanks to its relative territorial isolation.

Over time, both the Lombard Duchy of Beneventum and the Byzantine territories in southern Italy became extremely politically fragmented. The ascendancy of the Arabs across the Mediterranean caused serious problems for the Byzantines, who had to deploy most of their troops in Anatolia in order to defend the heartland of their empire. Following the reduction of the Byzantine military presence in southern Italy, the local nobles began governing their own lands and achieved a large degree of autonomy from the Byzantine Empire. Along the western coast of southern Italy, in particular, the local elites started to elect their own autonomous *duces*, or dukes, and to act independently from Byzantium. This process was not a true secession, since the new autonomous duchies emerging in Byzantine southern Italy never renounced their status of imperial territories. They were in essence Byzantine protectorates, only formally paying homage to the central authorities of the empire. The first such small state to emerge was the Duchy of Naples, which was ruled independently from Byzantium after 821. Naples, during the High Middle Ages, was the most flourishing commercial and agricultural centre of Campania, a region south of the papal territories centred on Rome and north of Sicily that had a great strategic importance. Initially, the Neapolitan dukes controlled a good portion of Campania on behalf of the Byzantine Empire and had to fight several campaigns against the Lombards established on the borders of their state. In 839, however, two smaller duchies seceded from the larger Duchy of Naples: the Duchy of Amalfi and the Duchy of Sorrento. The first of these soon became a flourishing naval and commercial centre, its merchants assuming control over the trade routes that connected Muslim northern Africa with southern Europe. Amalfi emerged as the first of the Italian Maritime Republics, autonomous urban centres holding naval power in the Mediterranean. Amalfi's merchants were superior to all their rivals in terms of naval capabilities and – thanks to their positive relations with the Muslim world – established a network of bases across the Mediterranean. Both the Duchy of Amalfi and the Duchy of Sorrento were located on the southern coastline of Campania; they had the same ambitions and contrasting interests, but in the end it was Amalfi that prevailed and emerged as a significant political player in southern Italy. In 839, another small state became independent from the larger Duchy of Naples: the Duchy of Gaeta. Located on the northern coastline of Campania, Gaeta was placed between the major cities of Rome and Naples. Like Amalfi, Gaeta soon transformed itself into a Maritime Republic and started to play a significant role in the commercial activities around the central Mediterranean. The city became Rome's primary supply port and thus started to enjoy the political protection of the papacy.

As a result of the events described above, the Byzantine territories in southern Italy became increasingly weak and fragmented. Nevertheless, the Lombards could not take advantage of this situation since their territories also experienced major secessions. In 851, after several years of civil war caused by a succession crisis, a large part of the Lombard territories in southern Italy (the richest ones, having access to the sea) seceded from the Duchy of Beneventum and proclaimed their independence as the Principality of Salerno. The two Lombard states of southern Italy were constantly at war with each other for most of their history, thus becoming increasingly weak militarily. In 900, another portion of the Duchy of Beneventum seceded and proclaimed its independence as the Principality of Capua, controlling the most fertile area of Campania's plain and thereby becoming an important agricultural state. By 900, due to these complex political changes, continental southern Italy comprised eight different political entities: the territories under direct Byzantine control, the Duchy of Naples, Duchy of Amalfi, Duchy of Sorrento, Duchy of Gaeta, Duchy of Beneventum, Principality of Salerno and Principality of Capua. The political situation in Sicily was completely different, it having been conquered by the Arabs, who defeated and expelled the Byzantines in 827. The Arabs gradually established a firm grip on the island, transforming it into the main base for their piratical raids, which were conducted across the Mediterranean and resulted – during 847 – in the Arab sacking of Rome. In 948, Sicily was transformed into an Emirate and started to be ruled by a powerful Muslim dynasty. After their conquest of Sicily, the Arabs tried to establish a foothold on continental southern Italy in 847 by attacking Byzantine territorial possessions in Apulia. They were able to conquer the important city of Bari and to establish a new Emirate there, but this was short-lived since in 871 it was destroyed by a powerful Christian alliance that comprised Holy Roman Emperor Louis II, Byzantine naval forces and Lombard military contingents from Beneventum, Salerno and Capua. In 982, the Arab Emirate of Sicily tried to invade continental southern Italy by landing troops in Calabria, but once again faced by a serious Muslim menace, the Christian states of southern Italy temporarily put aside their differences and formed an anti-Muslim alliance. During the ensuing conflict, the allied troops of Holy Roman Emperor Otto II and the Duchy of Beneventum were defeated by the Arabs at the Battle of Capo Colonna, but by the end of the campaign the Muslims had renounced their invasion plans. The closing years of the

The Norman Conquest of Southern Italy 77

Norman infantryman armed with single-handed falchion. (*Photo and copyright by Les Guerriers du Moyen-Age*)

Norman infantryman armed with double-handed falchion. (*Photo and copyright by Les Guerriers du Moyen-Age*)

tenth century were particularly chaotic for southern Italy, with the various local states resuming their usual internecine warfare in spite of the presence of the Arab menace. Both the Byzantines and the Lombards were becoming increasingly weak and thus – in addition to the Arabs – the Holy Roman Empire (that controlled northern Italy) also started to have plans for the annexation of southern Italy.

According to the available primary sources, the first Norman knights who visited southern Italy were pilgrims who – during their return journey from the Holy Land – crossed Apulia and settled in Salerno for some time during 999. While the Normans were in the Principality of Salerno, the capital of the Lombard state was attacked by a fleet of Arab pirates which, as was common practice at the time, demanded the payment of an annual tribute by the militarily weak Lombard princes. The Norman knights, seeing that the local population feared the Muslims, decided to attack the Arabs and easily defeated the pirates. The Lombard authorities, impressed by the combat skills of the Normans, asked them to stay in Salerno to serve as professional soldiers. The knights refused and returned to their homeland, but promised that they would tell their compatriots in Normandy about the potential for lucrative military service in Salerno. Before these events, southern Italy was already well known to the Normans, since they had a special veneration for Michael the Archangel, and an important shrine dedicated to him was located at Monte Gargano in Apulia. Many Norman knights visited this religious site every year and came into contact with the local Byzantine authorities. These, like the Lombards of Salerno, greatly appreciated the military skills of the Normans. After 999, small groups of Norman *milites* started to come to southern Italy, where they offered their services to both the Lombard rulers and Byzantine authorities. However, these first adventurers soon understood that their employers were extremely weak from a military point of view and that some of southern Italy's richest lands could be easily conquered. During the years 1009–22, southern Italy was ravaged by a large-scale conflict that saw the Lombards – temporarily united under the leadership of a warlord named Melus – fighting the Byzantines for possession of Apulia. During this war, the Lombards employed significant numbers of Norman mercenaries, who were encouraged by the Pope to fight against the Byzantine forces. The conflict ended without causing major changes to the status quo, except for one: in 1022, a group of Norman mercenaries, commanded by Gilbert Drengot, was able to occupy the County of Ariano – which was part of the Duchy of Beneventum – and to establish the first permanent Norman base in southern Italy.

During the following years, the Norman fighters, now guided by Ranulf Drengot, served in the various local conflicts of southern Italy, being employed by the Lombard princes who fought among themselves and also by the Duke of Naples. In 1030,

Sergius IV of Naples, in exchange for their military services, assigned to Ranulf Drengot and his followers the rich Neapolitan County of Aversa. The Normans soon transformed Aversa into an impressive military stronghold and started to act as autonomous rulers instead of being loyal vassals of Sergius IV. In 1038, after more Norman knights came to Aversa to build a new Norman homeland in southern Italy, Ranulf Drengot attacked and conquered the Lombard Principality of Capua, transforming it into a protectorate. A few months after the Normans conquered Capua, the Byzantines launched a large military campaign with the objective of seizing Sicily from the Arabs. The Lombard leaders of Beneventum and Salerno also contributed to the Byzantine war effort, sending a contingent of 300 Norman *milites* from Aversa who included three brothers of the Hauteville family: William, Drogo and Humphrey. These earned a strong military reputation during the ensuing campaign, despite the eventual defeat of the Byzantines; William, in particular, assumed the nickname of Bras-de-Fer, or Iron Arm, after single-handedly killing the Arab Emir of Syracuse. In 1041 and 1042, having seen that the Byzantines were quite weak due to their failed campaign in Sicily, the Normans invaded Apulia and occupied a good part of it. They formed a temporary alliance with the Lombards and obtained several victories over the Byzantines. Thanks to the success of his leadership, William Hauteville received the title of Count of Apulia and married the daughter of the Duke of Sorrento. Within a few years, the Normans had become the leading military power in southern Italy and were now ready to conquer the whole region from the local rulers who had previously employed them as mercenaries. However, the County of Aversa, ruled by the Drengot family, and the County of Apulia, under the Hautevilles, remained separate political entities.

In 1046, another two Norman warlords came to southern Italy: Richard Drengot in Aversa and Robert of Hauteville (nicknamed Guiscard, or The Cunning) in Apulia. By 1052, the Hauteville family had conquered much of Calabria – the conquest of which was progressively completed during the following years – from the Byzantines, meaning the Byzantine presence in southern Italy had been greatly reduced. Ruling from their capital of Melfi, the Normans of Apulia were becoming increasingly powerful and started to be perceived as a serious menace by the two major powers that dominated northern and central Italy: the Holy Roman Empire and the Pope. During 1053, Pope Leo IX formed a large anti-Norman alliance with the objective of expelling them from southern Italy. The anti-Hauteville front comprised Holy Roman Emperor Henry III – who sent 700 elite Swabian knights to the Pope – as well as the Duchy of Beneventum, Duchy of Gaeta, Duchy of Amalfi and papal military forces. Against the odds, despite their numerical inferiority, the Normans of Apulia were able to defeat Leo IX and his large army at the Battle of Civitate. The Norman knights obtained a complete victory, even being able to capture the Pope, who was forced

Norman peasant infantryman. (*Photo and copyright by Les Guerriers du Moyen-Âge*)

Norman peasant infantryman. The foot soldiers of the feudal levies did not wear any form of personal protection, except for a shield and sometimes a simple helmet. (*Photo and copyright by Les Guerriers du Moyen-Age*)

Norman peasant infantryman. The foot soldiers of the feudal levies used polearms that derived from the working tools of the contemporary peasants, like the one shown here. (*Photo and copyright by Les Guerriers du Moyen-Age*)

to recognize the legitimacy of all the Norman conquests in southern Italy. Following the Battle of Civitate, the Normans became the guardians of the papacy and transformed the Duchy of Beneventum into a protectorate (which was officially annexed by the Normans in 1078). By transforming themselves from the worst enemies to the main allies of the papacy, the Normans obtained the political legitimacy that they needed to complete the conquest of southern Italy. While the Hauteville family consolidated its power over Apulia and expanded north across the mountain region of Abruzzo, the Drengots gradually augmented their territorial domains. In 1059, the Principality of Capua was officially annexed to the County of Aversa, while in 1064 the Duchy of Gaeta became Drengot territory.

In 1061, the Pope, long having wished to free Sicily from the Arabs, gave Robert Guiscard the new title of Duke of Sicily and assigned him the daunting task of invading the island. Robert saw this as a great opportunity, since by conquering Sicily he would become stronger than his Drengot rivals. Norman

Norman peasant infantryman armed with flail, an agricultural tool used for separating grains from their husks. (*Photo and copyright by Les Guerriers du Moyen-Age*)

forces landed in Sicily in May 1061 and were swiftly able to conquer the important city of Messina. However, it soon became apparent that the Norman conquest of Sicily would be a long and difficult process: the Arabs, despite being fragmented into a series of local micro-states, organized a very strong resistance. After years of campaigning, during which they suffered several defeats, the Normans conquered the capital of Muslim Sicily, Palermo, on 7 January 1072. They continued fighting in Sicily, albeit with lesser intensity, until 1086, when they occupied the major port city of Syracuse. Nevertheless, the Norman conquest of Sicily was completed only in 1091 when the last Arab stronghold of Noto fell. During that same year, a Norman expedition occupied Malta and annexed it to the domains of the Hauteville family. While most of his forces fought in Sicily, Robert Guiscard continued to expand his possessions in continental southern Italy. In 1068, the remaining Byzantine territories in southern Italy, centred on Bari, were attacked by the Normans. Bari was finally conquered in 1071 after a bloody siege, ending forever the Byzantine presence in Italy. The Duchy of Amalfi was annexed without a fight in 1073, having been without a legitimate ruler. The Principality of Salerno was invaded in 1076, the capital of the last surviving Lombard state being captured after a difficult siege of eight months in 1077. After conquering Salerno, Robert Guiscard easily occupied the small Duchy of Sorrento and then besieged Naples from 1077–78. Although unable to take the city, he transformed it into a protectorate. The Duchy of Naples was formally absorbed into the Norman territorial possessions only during 1137, after all the Norman lands of southern Italy had been unified into the Kingdom of Sicily in 1130. In 1129, after it had become apparent that the Hauteville family was too strong for them, the members of the Drengot family accepted to become vassals of their rivals, meaning all their lands were included into the newly created Kingdom of Sicily in 1130.

Chapter 7

The Norman Contribution to the First Crusade

In 1095, the energetic Pope Urban II spent several months travelling across Italy and France in order to re-assert the authority of the papacy after the intricate political events involving Pope Gregory VII and Holy Roman Emperor Henry IV. Urban II wanted to carry on the Gregorian Reform and had an ambitious agenda, the main objective of which was achieving the reunification of the Eastern Church with the Western Church, thereby ending the fracture caused by the Great Schism of 1054. In March 1095, at Piacenza, a council of ecclesiastics and laymen of the Roman Catholic Church took place, at which the Pope met ambassadors sent by the Byzantine Emperor Alexius I Comnenus who described to the synodal assembly the situation that their state was enduring. The Byzantine envoys explained to the most important members of the Western Church how the Seljuk Turks from the steppes of Central Asia were in the process of invading the southern Balkans from Anatolia, menacing the imperial city of Byzantium. The arrival of the Turks would have been accompanied by widespread massacres of Christian civilians, as had already happened in Anatolia after the Battle of Manzikert (a great victory achieved by the Seljuks over the Byzantines in 1071). Due to their military weakness, caused by the long wars fought against the Muslim Fatimids of Egypt and the Christian Normans of southern Italy, the Byzantines were in no condition to organize an effective resistance against the Seljuks. Seeing no other alternative, Alexius I had decided to ask for help in Western Europe, where he hoped that the Christians would decide to assist him by sending troops. The Byzantine Emperor had been excommunicated by Gregory VII several years before, but his relationship with the new Pope, Urban II, had been generally good since the latter became pontifex in 1088.

After hearing full details of the difficult situation faced by the Byzantine Empire, the Pope organized a new council in France during which he asked the local aristocracy to assemble a military expedition for the defence of Byzantine lands. The council took place at Clermont, in central France, in November 1097. In medieval Western Europe, the Kingdom of France had the highest number of warlike nobles and knights, who, especially during the eleventh century, spent most of their time fighting against each other and thus had a very violent lifestyle. They lived in massive castles and showed very little respect for the authority of their monarch or that of

Norman peasant infantryman armed with wooden mace. (*Photo and copyright by Milites Pagenses*)

Norman peasant infantryman equipped with two-handed falchion. (*Photo and copyright by Les Guerriers du Moyen-Age*)

the local Church. They treated commoners very harshly and were interested only in plundering the lands of their enemies. Urban II understood that these warlike feudal warlords represented a great military resource for the Christian world, since they were skilled warriors who loved fighting. All the French nobles needed was holy cause to campaign for, possibly far away from their homeland, which had already been devastated by too many feudal wars. Religious zeal was strong among the French knights, most of whom were true believers. Indeed, many of them feared that their violent lifestyle could lead their souls to damnation after death and thus were in search of a way to purify themselves of their many sins. At Clermont, in front of the most important aristocrats of France, Urban II proclaimed the Truce of God, an official decree by the Church that prohibited fighting among feudal lords for a specific period of time. After this, the Pope invited the warlike nobles to turn their attention and energy away from feudal conflicts in order to defend the survival of their faith in other areas of the world. He described how the Seljuk Turks had invaded Byzantine Anatolia and reached the Mediterranean, becoming a menace for the Christian world. The nomads of the steppes had killed or enslaved thousands of Christian civilians, devastating religious sites and slaughtering many members of the clergy. After having impressed his audience with his words, Urban II issued a call to arms: all Christian people of whatever social condition – nobles or commoners – were asked to go to the aid of their Christian brothers in the Byzantine Empire. The ensuing conflict, according to the Pope's words, would be a holy war: its main objective would not be that of simply defending the Byzantine Empire, but of reconquering the Byzantine lands taken by the Muslims during the previous centuries. In practice, Urban II proposed to organize a massive military expedition directed against the Holy Land for the reconquest of Jerusalem. The Pope promised immediate absolution from all sins to all those who died on the way to the Holy Land or in battle against the Muslims. His political plan was extremely clear: he wanted to channel the bellicosity of the Christian aristocrats towards a holy cause in order to exert a renewed influence over the Christians of Eastern Europe. Private warfare between feudal lords was a plague for a country like the Kingdom of France, and thus Urban II was sure that his unexpected initiative would be well received by the Capetians who ruled France. By promising an eternal reward to those knights and commoners who marched to the Holy Land, the Pope was sure that it would be possible to assemble a very large military force. However, the Byzantine envoys who had been sent to Piacenza a few months before had not exactly been asking for this. Alexius I had only hoped that the Pope could send him some mercenaries recruited from Western Europe, not an entire army of Franks moved by religious zeal. The response of the aristocrats who were present at Clermont to Urban II's call to arms was spontaneous and enthusiastic: they cried '*Deus vult*' ('God wills it') in front of the Pope, expressing their will to leave their homeland for the glory of religion. They soon became known as Crusaders, from the Latin words *cruce signati* (bearers of the cross), since they started to wear crosses on their clothing and armour as a mark of distinction. Urban II hoped that the knights and commoners would fight together against the common enemy represented by the Muslims, forming a single Christian army that would be aimed at Byzantium. In the end, however, this did not happen, since two separate expeditions were organized. One, conducted by commoners, was the so-called People's Crusade; the other, organized by the most important aristocrats of Western Europe, became known as the Princes' Crusade. The two expeditions are collectively known as the First Crusade.

The People's Crusade was organized without the official permission of the Papacy by a charismatic monk and powerful orator named Peter the Hermit, who came from the French city of Amiens. Peter was well known in every corner of France for travelling around the countryside on a donkey and dressing in simple clothing. He was a true predicator, a poor monk who lived among the peasants and experienced their humble way of life. Peter preached the crusade throughout northern France and Flanders, claiming to have been appointed to do so by Christ himself. The charismatic hermit eventually assembled a large number of peasants and low-ranking knights, who made up a giant band of illiterate pilgrims with no idea of how to reach the Holy Land but who decided to launch a crusade on their own. The peasants in northern France and Flanders had been afflicted by drought and famine for many years before 1096; as a result, these commoners envisioned Peter's crusade as an opportunity to escape from the hardships of their daily life. Being very superstitious, they were also influenced in their decision to go to the Holy Land by a series of natural events that were perceived as a divine blessing for their movement: during the last weeks of 1095, for example, a lunar eclipse and the passing of a comet took place. Around 100,000 people, including women and children, were under Peter's orders when the People's Crusade began in the spring of 1096. Moving along the Rhine, they destroyed most of the Jewish communities encountered along the way in a series of unprecedentedly large pogroms. Thousands of Jews, who had lived and prospered in the Rhineland for centuries, were killed without reason or were forced to become Christians. The largest massacres took place in Worms and Mainz. The religious zeal of the Crusaders made them consider the Jews as enemies of the true religion because – centuries before – their ancestors had killed Christ.

After reaching the city of Cologne on 12 April 1096, Peter gathered his army and stopped in Germany in order to gather more supporters from the local communities of peasants. Some of his French followers, however, continued the march and crossed

Norman archer wearing Phrygian cap. (*Photo and copyright by Milites Pagenses*)

Norman archer. (*Photo and copyright by Historia Aquitanorum*)

the border between the Holy Roman Empire and the Kingdom of Hungary. The latter controlled a vast portion of the northern Balkans and was located between Germany and the Byzantine Empire. When this first group of Crusaders reached the Byzantine border at Belgrade, under the leadership of Walter Sans Avoir, the local authorities temporarily denied them permission to enter Byzantine territory. After having enlarged his army with many German commoners, Peter marched to the Danube, where his forces were split in two: some of the Crusaders decided to continue by boat down the river, but most of them preferred continuing overland and thus entered Hungarian territory. In Zemun, not far from the border with the Byzantine Empire, a serious incident took place between the newly arrived Crusaders and the local Hungarian population, which led to the storming of the city and the killing of over 4,000 Hungarians (mostly civilians). The commoners then moved on Belgrade, which was evacuated by the Byzantines in order to avoid further massacres. The city was pillaged and burned by the Crusaders, who continued their march across Byzantine territory. The armed pilgrims were more violent and destructive than an invading army, raiding the countryside in search of supplies and killing everyone who tried to stop them. Byzantine troops were forced to intervene to restore order, attacking the Crusaders and killing almost 10,000 of them. After this clash, the remaining 30,000 armed pilgrims were escorted by Byzantine forces to Byzantium. Alexius I had no idea how to employ this army of peasants that had reached his lands, rightly fearing that Peter's men could cause more devastation to his territory. Consequently, he quickly ferried them across the Bosporus to the Anatolian coastline. Knowing that most of them had no military capability, he hoped that the Seljuks would soon slaughter them. Once in Anatolia, the commoners began pillaging all the urban settlements they encountered until they reached Nicomedia. Here, Peter the Hermit completely lost control over his army, with two new leaders being elected: one for the French and another for the Germans. The Germans, by now numbering around 6,000, marched on Xerigordos and captured the fortress there. Soon, however, they were besieged in the stronghold by the Seljuks. A lack of water led to the Crusaders surrendering, and they were all captured or enslaved by the Turks. The main Crusader army, now consisting of approximately 20,000 French, built a large camp not far from Nicaea for women and children to rest while the armed men patrolled the surrounding countryside in search of supplies. Three miles from the camp, along a road that entered a narrow and wooded valley, the Seljuks had assembled a large cavalry army of mounted archers. These ambushed the Crusaders and swiftly massacred them with a rain of deadly arrows. The camp was soon invested by the Turks, who killed many women and children but spared those who surrendered. The People's Crusade thus ended in complete failure due to its complete lack of

Norman crossbowman (left) and archer (right). (*Photo and copyright by Historia Aquitanorum*)

Norman archer wearing peasant headgear made of wicker. (*Photo and copyright by Les Guerriers du Moyen-Age*)

military organization. Having no campaigning experience, the commoners had been seriously damaged by logistical problems and had not even been able to reach the Holy Land. Only 3,000 of them survived, being transported back to Byzantium. Clearly, religious zeal was not enough to make a crusade a successful expedition.

Compared with the People's Crusade, which was little more than a disorganized mass pilgrimage, the Princes' Crusade was a well-planned military expedition. Being directed by the papacy, it started in August 1096 and consisted of four distinct armies that took different routes to Byzantium. According to modern estimates, around 100,000 people participated in the Princes' Crusade: 7,000 knights, 35,000 foot soldiers (mostly feudal peasant levies) and 60,000 civilian non-combatants (including women and children). The spiritual leader of the expedition was Adhemar of Le Puy, one of the most influential French bishops, who had been chosen by the Pope because of his military competence and great experience. There were many military leaders of the crusade, most of them from the dominant aristocratic families of France: Raymond IV of Toulouse, Godfrey of Bouillon, Baldwin of Boulogne, Hugh of Vermandois, Stephen II of Blois, Robert II of Flanders and Robert Curthose. Raymond IV, Count of Toulouse, was the most powerful noble in southern France; Godfrey of Bouillon, Duke of Lower Lorraine, was one of France's most experienced military commanders and had been a loyal supporter of Emperor Henry IV; and Baldwin of Boulogne, Count of Verdun, was Godfrey of Bouillon's younger brother. Hugh of Vermandois, Count of Vermandois, was the younger brother of the King of France, Philip I; Stephen II of Blois, Count of Blois and Chartres, was one of the most powerful aristocrats of northern France and had married William the Conqueror's daughter, Adela of Normandy; Robert II, Count of Flanders, controlled one of Europe's richest regions, located between France and Germany; and Robert Curthose, Duke of Normandy, was the eldest son of William the Conqueror and the older brother of the King of England, William II. In addition to these leaders, there also were two more from southern Italy: Bohemond of Taranto and Tancred of Hauteville. Bohemond was the son of Robert Guiscard (the leader of the Norman adventurers who had conquered southern Italy) and was the Prince of Taranto, while Tancred was a nephew of Bohemond and an ambitious young leader. Bohemond of Taranto was a very experienced military commander, having fought under his father when Robert Guiscard tried to invade the Byzantine Empire in 1081. During the latter campaign, at the Battle of Dyrrachium, Bohemond and his father decisively defeated Alexius I and his Byzantine troops. The Norman invasion of the southern Balkans later ended up in failure, but the Byzantine Emperor never forgot the defeat that he had suffered at the hands of the Normans from southern Italy. As a result, when Bohemond and Tancred joined the Princes' Crusade, Alexius I became increasingly concerned about the real intentions of the expedition. The Byzantines feared that the Normans had joined the crusade just to pursue their own political interests in an opportunistic way, to invade the southern Balkans. The main Crusader leaders were thus powerful French aristocrats who controlled large territorial possessions in Western Europe, and several of them were related to the Norman and Capetian royal families of England and France.

The Crusader forces were divided into four separate armies that followed different routes during their journey to the Holy Land. Godfrey of Bouillon and Baldwin of Boulogne crossed the Holy Roman Empire before entering the Kingdom of Hungary, where Baldwin had to be offered as a hostage to King Coloman of Hungary to guarantee the good conduct of Godfrey's troops. The Hungarians had become Christians only during the reign of Stephen I (1000–38) and did not have a great opinion of the Crusaders, fearing that their realm could be devastated by them as had already happened during the People's Crusade. Hughes of Vermandois departed from Paris and crossed France before descending into the Italian peninsula. He then sailed from Apulia across the Adriatic Sea to Dyrrachium. Raymond of Toulouse crossed the Alps and entered northern Italy, then marched along the western coastline of the Balkans (present-day Croatia) before reaching Dyrrachium. Bohemond of Taranto and Tancred of Hauteville assembled their forces in Apulia and then crossed the Adriatic; after disembarking on Byzantine territory, they advanced further into the heart of the southern Balkans. The four Crusader armies all headed for Byzantium, where they expected to receive provisions from Alexius I. In return for food and supplies, Alexius requested the western nobles swear fealty to him and promise to return to the Byzantine Empire any land recovered from the Seljuks. Thereafter, the Crusaders were ferried across the Bosporus by the Byzantine navy.

After entering Turkish territory, the Crusaders marched across Anatolia without encountering serious opposition. Their first target was the city of Nicaea, the capital of the Seljuk Sultanate of Rum. The Nicaeans had already defeated the People's Crusade and did not expect the arrival of another European expedition. Their monarch, Arslan, was campaigning against a local enemy in central Anatolia, meaning he was unready to stop the advance of the Crusaders. Nicaea was besieged by the whole Crusader force, with the objective of transforming it into their main logistical base in Anatolia. Arslan, having been informed of the attack on his capital, assembled all the troops that were at his disposal and advanced towards Nicaea. On 16 May 1097, the Turkish relief force attacked the Crusaders, but was defeated in a bloody night battle. Both sides suffered severe losses, but the Seljuk army had to leave Nicaea to its destiny. Following this battle, some Byzantine troops joined the besieging Crusaders. Indeed, Alexius I feared that after conquering the city,

Norman archer equipped with *cervelliere* helmet and padded aketon. (*Photo and copyright by Les Guerriers du Moyen-Age*)

Norman crossbowman. (*Photo and copyright by Historia Aquitanorum*)

the western knights would keep Nicaea for themselves. Following the arrival of the Byzantine soldiers, and being in a desperate situation, the defenders of Nicaea finally surrendered. However, they gave the city to the commander of the Byzantine troops and not to any of the Crusader leaders. Most of the latter were particularly unhappy about this, the Byzantines having forbidden the Crusaders from entering Nicaea in groups larger than ten men at a time. Tension started to grow between them and the Byzantines, especially as the Crusaders had suffered significant losses in taking the city. Alexius I gave the Crusaders money and rich gifts, hoping that this would be enough to placate their indignation. Eight days after Nicaea fell on 18 June, the Crusaders left to continue their 'liberation' of the Middle East from Muslim rule. They resumed their march in two columns: one, comprising some Byzantine troops, was commanded by Bohemond and formed the vanguard, while the other, comprising the best French troops, was led by Godfrey and formed the rearguard.

While the Crusaders reorganized themselves after the conquest of Nicaea, Arslan gathered a new and much larger army from his Seljuks. He then closely followed the movements of the Crusaders' vanguard, waiting for the right opportunity to lay an ambush. On 1 July, outside the settlement of Dorylaeum, Bohemond's Norman and Byzantine troops were surrounded by the Turks, who launched a surprise attack while Bohemond's men were in their newly built camp. The Crusader leaders had agreed that upon reaching Dorylaeum, their vanguard would stop and await the arrival of the rearguard. Initially, Bohemond's Normans suffered significant casualties, coming under a rain of arrows, but they soon mounted their horses and mounted counter-attacks against the fast-moving Seljuk horse archers. The Turks, however, were much faster than the heavy-armoured knights and could not be intercepted by them. The Seljuks then began riding into the enemy camp, cutting down large numbers of non-combatants and foot soldiers, who were unable to deploy in battle formation. At this point, to protect his infantrymen and civilians, Bohemond ordered his knights to dismount and form a defensive line. The foot soldiers and non-combatants were gathered in the centre of the camp, where they tried to support the *milites*. The Seljuks attacked in their traditional style, charging in and shooting volleys of arrows before quickly retreating. Being on foot, the Norman knights could no longer mount effective counter-attacks, and were thus obliged to play a passive tactical role. The Turkish arrows did little damage to the heavily armoured *milites*, but inflicted serious casualties among their horses, which were kept in the centre of the defensive formation. Being in an increasingly difficult situation, Bohemond sent messengers to Godfrey and the rearguard and tried to resist for as long as possible. He was forced back to the banks of the River Thymbris, where the marshy terrain slowed down the Seljuk assaults. The knights formed a circle around the foot soldiers and civilians, but small groups of them occasionally broke ranks and charged the enemy, only to be slaughtered by the Turks. The Turks were surprised by the strength of their opponents' armour, but controlled the battlefield and could move across it without hindrance since the Crusaders had no missile troops with which to respond to the Seljuk volleys of arrows. Just after midday, with the situation beginning to turn desperate for Bohemond, Godfrey's reinforcements started to reach the battlefield in small groups. After seven hours of fighting, Raymond arrived with a substantial number of *milites* and launched a surprise charge against one of the Seljuks' exposed flanks. This allowed the dispersed Crusaders to rally and form a well-organized line of battle. The *milites* rapidly deployed in offensive formation and launched a general charge against the Turks, with all the leading Crusader knights who were now on the battlefield taking part. The Seljuks were surprised by the violence and power of the charge, having never seen feudal cavalry in action before. Hundreds of unarmoured Turkish horse archers were slaughtered, especially after some more reinforcements under Adhemar of Le Puy arrived on the battlefield and invested the Seljuk camp. Being surrounded and having no more chance of victory, the Turks started to flee. The Battle of Dorylaeum, against all odds, thus ended in victory for the Crusaders. Soon after the end of the clash, they looted the enemy camp and captured the rich treasury of Arslan. The Seljuk ruler, being in no condition to fight another battle, burned and destroyed everything he left behind in his army's flight. His scorched earth tactics proved effective, as it was the middle of summer and the Crusaders had very few supplies with them in Anatolia. The local population did not consider the Crusaders as liberators, and thus did not help them by providing supplies. The Crusader army was extremely numerous and to keep moving needed a lot of water and food, but southern Anatolia was not particularly rich in either, being a very inhospitable land for an invading force.

After passing through the Cilician Gates, a strategic mountain pass connecting southern Anatolia with northern Syria, Baldwin and Tancred decided to break away from the main body of the Crusader army and set off towards Cilician Armenia. Also known as Lesser Armenia, this was a small state created around 1080 by Armenian refugees who were fleeing the Seljuk invasion of their homeland in the Caucasus (present-day Armenia). Cilician Armenia was located in south-western Anatolia, in an area covered by mountains that was of great strategic importance since it connected Anatolia with Syria and was not distant from the sea. As we have seen, among the various Crusader leaders, Baldwin and Tancred were more interested in conquering a region of the Holy Land for themselves in order to become major feudal lords, having few possessions of their own in Europe. In Cilician Armenia, the great majority of the local population consisted of Christians, who were ready to

Norman crossbowman equipped with cervelliere helmet and padded aketon. (*Photo and copyright by Les Guerriers du Moyen-Age*)

Norman crossbowman. (*Photo and copyright by Les Guerriers du Moyen-Age*)

support the Crusaders by supplying them with supplies and guides. After defeating the Seljuk garrison of Tarsus, Baldwin and Tancred were welcomed by the Armenian people. At that time, Cilician Armenia was fragmented into a series of minor states that were controlled by local rulers; these had been at war with the Turks for several years and thus welcomed the arrival of the Crusaders. Some Armenian rulers, however, soon realized that the Crusaders had come to rest and not just to free them from the Turks. Consequently, the Crusaders had to fight some minor clashes against groups of Armenians who were unhappy about their arrival. On 10 March 1098, after having occupied a good portion of Cilician Armenia, Baldwin assumed the title of Count of Edessa, establishing the first of the Crusader states of the Middle East. The occupation of Armenian lands located along the River Euphrates by Baldwin and Tancred secured an important source of supplies for the Crusaders, who finally started to control some territories of the Levant. The lands making up the new County of Edessa were not given back to the Byzantine Empire as promised by the Crusader leaders several months before. Until that moment, thanks to the success of the Crusaders, Alexius I had been able to reconquer a large portion of western Anatolia without employing significant numbers of his own troops. Following the Armenian campaign of Baldwin and Tancred, however, the situation started to change because the European warlords began keeping the newly conquered lands for themselves.

While these events took place in Cilician Armenia, the main Crusader army marched on to Antioch, one of the Middle East's most important and richest cities, situated midway between Byzantium and Jerusalem. Being well-fortified and having a large population, it had to be taken by the Crusaders if they wanted to continue their march across Syria. Upon reaching Antioch, the western leaders saw that it would be impossible for them to storm the city since its defences were too strong, so they started besieging Antioch in the hope of forcing it into capitulation without having to suffer severe losses. Once the siege began on 20 October 1097, the Crusaders soon started to experience serious difficulties. First of all, they did not have enough troops to surround the city, which was thus able to remain supplied. The army besieged Antioch for eight months without achieving anything, thousands of Crusaders dying from starvation since their supplies were not sufficient to sustain such a large army operating in a foreign country. Meanwhile, the Seljuk rulers of Aleppo and Damascus, two brothers who were at war with each other, sent separate relief armies against the Crusaders, but these were easily defeated. Understanding that the Crusaders were too weak to conquer Antioch, the Turks decided to put aside their political differences and raise a single relief army guided by a leader named Kerbogha. The Crusader leaders besieging Antioch spent much of their time quarrelling among themselves,

Norman crossbowman recharging his weapon.' (*Photo and copyright by Les Guerriers du Moyen-Age*)

Norman crossbowman with *chapel de fer* helmet and chainmail. (*Photo and copyright by Les Guerriers du Moyen-Age*)

since each of them planned to transform the city into one of his personal domains. Bohemond, in particular, was determined to gain control of Antioch since the city was the gateway to Syria. Stephen of Blois left the besieging army during the most difficult moment of the siege and informed Alexius I that the Byzantine cause in the Middle East was lost, since the other Crusader leaders had no intention to free any land for the Byzantines. Alexius had assembled an army to support the siege of Antioch and was marching through Anatolia when he was informed by Stephen about the actual intentions of the Crusaders. Now wishing them to be defeated by the Seljuks, the Byzantine Emperor returned to his capital without sending any reinforcements or supplies to the Crusaders. However, on 2 June, an Armenian traitor living inside Antioch – having been paid by Bohemond – opened one of the city gates, allowing a small party of Crusaders to enter. Seeing this, the Christian inhabitants of Antioch opened the other gates of the city to allow in the Crusaders. After months of suffering from starvation, the Crusaders then took revenge with acts of extreme violence after accessing the city, sacking and killing without mercy and also causing significant losses to the Christian civilians within Antioch. The citadel of the city, however, remained in Turkish hands and continued to resist thanks to its strong fortifications.

Two days later, on 4 June, the vanguard of Kerbogha's army of 40,000 men arrived outside Antioch. The Crusaders, taken by surprise, had to quickly improvise a defence of the city, but fortunately for them, the city walls had not been damaged during the siege. From 10 June, Kerbogha's soldiers assaulted Antioch's walls for four days from dawn until dusk. The Crusaders, despite being vastly outnumbered, managed to hold out. The city gates were barred to prevent desertions, and the civilian population was forced to support the Crusaders. Having been repulsed several times, the Turks halted their assaults and settled down to try and starve the Crusaders out. Morale inside Antioch soon plummeted, with hundreds of soldiers and civilians dying from starvation. Once again, the Crusaders did not have sufficient supplies with them, having poorly planned the logistical aspects of their campaign. Just when everything seemed lost, a peasant visionary who was with the Crusader army – named Peter Bartholomew – claimed that Saint Andrew had shown him the location of the Holy Lance that had pierced Christ on the cross. The Holy Lance was found exactly where Peter Bartholomew searched for it, which boosted the morale of the exhausted defenders. Having no more supplies left but being full of religious zeal, the Crusaders marched out of Antioch in four groups on 28 June to engage the enemy in a decisive – albeit desperate – pitched battle. Kerbogha did not stop the deployment of the enemy army, being confident that his forces could destroy it in battle. However, Kerbogha's troops contained large numbers of non-professional fighters, who

Norman mounted crossbowman. (*Photo and copyright by Les Guerriers du Moyen-Age*)

Norman mounted crossbowman wearing nasal helmet. (*Photo and copyright by Les Guerriers du Moyen-Age*)

launched a disorderly attack against the Crusaders as they deployed. The Crusaders, knowing that their destiny depended on this battle, charged the Muslim forces with violent desperation, quickly killing hundreds of them. Kerbogha's army was routed and fled Antioch, after which the remaining defenders of the citadel surrendered to the Crusaders. It was a complete victory for the Crusaders, and especially for Bohemond, who became the ruler of Antioch.

Bohemond was angry at Alexius I over his decision to abandon them to their fate, arguing that this invalidated all the Crusaders' oaths to him; as a result, following the conquest of Antioch, the Crusaders began to act independently from the Byzantines and the whole venture assumed a new nature. The western knights were now fighting to conquer the Holy Land for themselves, not to restore the Byzantine presence in the Middle East. After occupying Antioch, however, the Crusaders started quarrelling among themselves again, and remained immobile for several months. Now that the expedition had turned into a campaign of conquest, all the various leaders wanted to create their own personal states in the Middle East. The three main groups making up the Crusader army also had contrasting interests in Europe: the nobles of northern France hated those of southern France and had long planned to invade their lands; and the Norman nobles of southern Italy were considered by the French Crusaders to be mere pirates who simply wanted to become rich by plundering the Holy Land. While they discussed how best to continue the campaign, a plague broke out among the ranks of the Crusader army, killing hundreds of people (including Adhemar, who had tried to limit the personal ambitions of the various warlords and to keep the venture under the direct control of the Pope). By this time, the Crusaders were in no condition to continue their march across the Middle East, having remained in Antioch for so many months. They now had very few horses and – as usual – suffered from a chronic lack of supplies. The Muslim peasants in the countryside around Antioch refused to give them food, and all nearby areas had already been pillaged. Once again on the verge of starvation, at the beginning of 1099, the Crusaders had no choice but to resume their advance towards the heart of the Holy Land. Many knights and commoners were becoming impatient at the lack of progress and seemed ready to revolt against their leaders. Furthermore, time was working in favour of the Muslims, who were able to improve their defences in the Holy Land.

When the Crusaders left Antioch, Bohemond remained in the city as the first Prince of Antioch. The new Crusader state created by Bohemond, the Principality of Antioch, later flourished. In order to receive enough supplies from the sea, the Crusader army resumed its advance by moving along the Mediterranean coast of the Holy Land. They encountered little resistance during this phase of the expedition, the local rulers of the area between northern Syria and Palestine preferring to make peace with them and furnish them with supplies rather than see their lands devastated. After Bohemond remained in Antioch, the internal hierarchy of the Crusader leaders changed significantly. Robert Curthose and Tancred agreed to become vassals of Raymond IV of Toulouse, in the hope of receiving lands from him in the Holy Land in exchange for their military services. Raymond was by then the strongest and wealthiest of the Crusader leaders marching across the Levant. Tancred had tried to obtain some lands in Cilician Armenia, but without success; he had then attempted to become Bohemond's right arm in Antioch, but had not received the political importance that he strongly desired. As a result, the ambitious

Norman noble allied himself with his former rival, Raymond, who hated his uncle Bohemond. Godfrey of Bouillon, now counting on the support of his brother, who had become Prince of Edessa, emerged as an alternative leader to Raymond. During the march towards Jerusalem, Raymond decided to take the major city of Tripoli and to transform it into the capital of a new Crusader state north of Palestine. To achieve his objective, however, he first had to besiege the fortified city of Arqa in northern Lebanon. While Raymond was fighting at Arqa, Godfrey and Robert of Flanders continued their march southwards in the hope of being the first to reach Jerusalem. Tancred, who had been loyal to Raymond until that moment, decided to follow Godfrey and Robert, believing that the new Crusader state that was to be created in Tripoli would never be assigned to him. Raymond's siege of Arqa was a complete failure, the city remaining in Muslim hands.

With tension growing among the Crusader leaders due to their internal rivalries, any military setback – even if only temporary – risked provoking the collapse of the whole expedition. Following Adhemar's death, there had been no real spiritual leader of the Crusade. The discovery of the Holy Lance had not resolved this problem, since there had been public accusations of fraud among the opposing clerical factions that participated in the expedition. Peter Bartholomew, the man who discovered the relic, was challenged to an ordeal by fire; he underwent it and died from his wounds after days of terrible agony. This discredited the Holy Lance as a fake and also undermined Raymond's political authority, since he had been one of the main proponents of its authenticity. While these events took place among the Crusaders, a new conflict broke out among the Muslims. Shortly before the arrival of the western knights in Anatolia, Jerusalem and most of Palestine had been occupied by the Seljuks, who temporarily defeated the local Fatimid garrisons. After the Crusaders crushed most of the Turks' military power, however, the Fatimids took advantage of the situation to launch a campaign of reconquest in Palestine from their Egyptian territories. A few months before the arrival of the Crusaders in front of its walls, the Holy City of Jerusalem was reoccupied by the Fatimids, who expelled the Seljuks from most of Palestine. The Fatimids then tried to make a deal with the Crusaders by promising freedom of passage to any pilgrim heading to the Holy Land in exchange for a promise not to invade Fatimid territory. The offer, however, was promptly refused by the Crusaders, who were by now convinced that it would be quite easy to capture Jerusalem. The city had a new Fatimid governor, named Iftikhar ad-Daula, who became increasingly worried about the imminent arrival of the Crusaders and thus decided to expel all the Christian inhabitants from Jerusalem, fearing that they may help the westerners during an eventual siege. The Fatimid commander knew very well that the forces under his direct control were too small to meet the invaders in

Norman peasant infantryman armed with staff sling. (*Photo and copyright by Milites Pagenses*)

a pitched battle. In addition, he had been impressed by the accounts of the previous clashes fought between the Crusaders – described as 'wild beasts' because of their ferocity in combat – and the Seljuks. Consequently, Iftikhar ad-Daula prepared his troops for a long siege. His plan was very simple: keep the Crusaders outside the walls of Jerusalem for several months, causing them to run out of supplies and to die of starvation. To achieve his objective, he reinforced the defences of the Holy City and poisoned most of the wells surrounding Jerusalem.

Norman peasant infantryman armed with staff sling. (*Photo and copyright by Les Guerriers du Moyen-Age*)

Upon reaching Tripoli, the Crusader leaders were convinced that they would be obliged to fight in order to occupy the city. Contrary to their expectations, however, the governor of the city surrendered without a fight. He provided the knights with a number of fine horses and promised that he would convert to Christianity if they defeated his Fatimid enemies. During the spring of 1099, the Crusaders advanced rapidly towards Palestine. They reached Beirut on 9 May, and on 23 May they passed Tyre, without meeting opposition from local troops. They thus entered Palestine without further fighting, reaching the city of Ramla, that had been hastily abandoned by its inhabitants. Ramla was soon transformed into their main base by the Crusader leaders, who started planning their next move to free those area of Palestine where Jesus was said to have lived. On 6 June, Godfrey sent Tancred with a token force to Bethlehem, which he occupied very easily without losses. Tancred had the great personal satisfaction of placing his banner over the Church of the Nativity, one of the most important Christian sites of the Holy Land. On 7 June, after a short march, the main Crusader army arrived in view of Jerusalem. For many of the Crusaders, this was a dream come true, a moment of their lives that they would never forget. The Fatimids were expecting their arrival and had prepared for a long siege. Additional supplies had been stored inside Jerusalem, an elite force of 400 cavalrymen coming from Egypt had reinforced the local garrison and all the trees around the Holy City had been cut down. The latter move was a very intelligent one: to build the siege machines needed to assault Jerusalem, the Crusaders would now be obliged to search for large amounts of wood far from the besieged city, thereby causing them serious delays. Jerusalem was guarded by a defensive wall that stretched for 4km, and was 3m thick and 15m high. These were impressive defences for the standards of the time. Five major gates opened in the walls, each of which was protected by a pair of towers.

The Crusaders, soon after starting the siege, divided their forces in two: one part, commanded by Godfrey, camped in front of Jerusalem's northern side, while the other, under Raymond's orders, camped to the south of the Holy City. By attacking from two sides at the same time, they hoped to take the city more easily. The Crusaders launched their first frontal assault on 13 June. However, at this time they had no access to wood for the construction of siege equipment and thus attacked Jerusalem's walls with the single ladder that they had been able to build. Such logistical unpreparedness was a perfect example of the many improvisations that the Crusaders had to make during an expedition that had so far been more successful than expected. By attacking with a single ladder at a single point of the walls, they had no hope of success. They did fight with great courage during the assault, and one of them – a knight named Rainbold – even managed to scale the ladder and gain a foothold on the walls, but the attack was eventually repulsed with significant losses. Religious zeal was not enough to take

Early form of nasal helmet. (*Photo and copyright by Historia Aquitanorum*)

Detail of the hood of chainmail that was worn under the helmet. (*Photo and copyright by Historia Aquitanorum*)

a well-fortified city like Jerusalem. Demoralized but not defeated, the Crusaders pulled back to their siege lines and decided not to launch any further assaults until they found enough wood to build proper siege machines, not just a few ladders. Without at least two siege towers, it was impossible to attack the defences from the north and the south at the same moment. In this phase of the siege, the Crusaders faced many difficulties, including lack of water and shortages of food, the result of the Fatimids' scorched earth tactics. Palestine's summer temperatures did not help the besiegers, who were not used to such heat. At the end of June, the Crusader leaders were informed that a large Fatimid relief force was entering southern Palestine from Egypt. They thus decided to act quickly and seize Jerusalem before the arrival of the enemy army. The strategic situation of the besiegers was a very difficult one: they were camped in an arid countryside, where no natural resources were available, and they could not try to blockade Jerusalem as they had done with Antioch because the Holy City was simply too large. Previous clashes during the expedition, together with illness and desertions, had greatly reduced the strength of the Crusaders, who by now numbered just 12,000 men, of whom only 1,500 were knights.

On 17 June, with the Crusader army seeming to be on the verge of annihilation, Genoese ships under the command of Guglielmo Embriaco arrived in the port of Jaffa. The Genoese sailors came to the aid of the Crusaders at the most decisive moment of the campaign, providing them with skilled engineers capable of building effective siege machines as well as with sufficient amounts of timber (stripped from the ships, which were hauled ashore). After the arrival of the Genoese vessels, the besiegers' morale was also raised by a priest named Peter Desiderius, who claimed to have had a vision of Adhemar of Le Puy instructing the Crusaders to march in barefoot procession around Jerusalem's walls, after which the city would fall (as had happened during the Biblical episode of the siege of Jericho). On 8 July, the Crusaders performed the procession exactly as they had been instructed by Peter Desiderius, ending it on the Mount of Olives where the various factions existing among the besiegers arrived at a public rapprochement. After the arrival of the Genoese vessels, in almost three weeks, the Crusaders built some of the most effective siege equipment ever employed during the eleventh century. This included two massive wheel-mounted siege towers, a battering ram with an iron-clad head, several scaling ladders and numerous portable wattle screens. The attackers could now defend themselves from the arrows of the enemy, and had two siege towers in order to attack Jerusalem from two different points. The Fatimids were impressed by the siege equipment of the enemy but were ready to respond with their mangonel artillery mounted on the city walls. The assault on Jerusalem began on 13 July: Raymond's troops, attacking from the south, made little progress and suffered severe losses; but those under Godfrey, attacking from the north, soon started to push – slowly but steadily – the Fatimid defenders away from the walls. At the end of the first day of fighting, however, the walls were still in Muslim hands. On 15 July, the Crusaders resumed their attack with increasing determination, seeing that the Fatimid resistance was weakening. The inner rampart of the northern wall, after some violent fighting, was finally occupied by Godfrey's knights. Thereafter, the Fatimid soldiers panicked and abandoned Jerusalem's walls. The Crusaders then entered the city and started to massacre all the Muslim and Jewish civilians they came across, showing no mercy. The Fatimid troops fled to the Temple Mount, with Tancred and his knights in close pursuit. The Norman leader reached the Temple Mount before the defenders could establish a new position, his men hastily slaughtering many of the surviving Fatimids. The few survivors took refuge in the Al-Aqsa Mosque, being determined to fight to the last man. At this point, however, Tancred called a halt to his attack and offered his personal protection to the Fatimids who were in the mosque in exchange for their immediate surrender. While these events took place in the northern part of Jerusalem, to the south the Fatimid troops resisted strongly against the attacks of Raymond until they were informed that the northern wall had fallen. At that point they left their defensive positions and moved to the Holy City's citadel, allowing Raymond to enter Jerusalem. Iftikhar ad-Daula, seeing that his situation was hopeless, decided to make a deal with Raymond, surrendering the citadel in return for being granted safe passage to Ascalon. After the last Fatimid troops gave up the fight, the slaughter of civilians continued for the rest of the day. Thousands of Muslims, including many women and children, fell victim to the fury of the Crusaders. Many Jews, who had taken refuge in their synagogue, were killed when the building was burnt down by the Crusaders. On the following day, Tancred's prisoners who had surrendered in the Al-Aqsa Mosque were also massacred without reason. The few Muslims and Jews who were not killed by the Crusaders fled Jerusalem in haste or were taken prisoner to be ransomed. According to eyewitness accounts, the streets of the Holy City were literally running with blood, with some 40,000 civilians slaughtered.

On 17 July, a council was held among the Crusader leaders to discuss who would be crowned as the new King of Jerusalem. After some vibrant discussions, Godfrey of Bouillon – whose troops had played a fundamental role during the siege – was named Advocatus Sancti Sepulchri (Defender of the Holy Sepulchre). The experienced warlord refused to be named king in the city where Christ had died, showing his respect for religion. Arnulf of Chocques, one of Raymond's most loyal followers, was elected the first Latin Patriarch of Jerusalem on 1 August; four days later, after consulting surviving inhabitants of the city, he discovered the holy relic of the True Cross. Urban II, the inventor of the Crusade, died on 29 July 1099, a few days before

Nice example of a mask helmet. (*Photo and copyright by Les Guerriers du Moyen-Age*)

he could be informed of Jerusalem's recapture. Soon after the Crusaders consolidated their presence in the Holy City, Fatimid ambassadors arrived in Jerusalem and ordered them to leave the city as soon as possible. Godfrey, who had not forgotten that a large enemy army was on its way from Egypt, prepared his remaining forces for the last battle of the expedition. He marched towards Ascalon with most of the other leaders, except for Raymond of Toulouse and Robert of Normandy, who left Jerusalem a day after the main Crusader army had marched against the enemy. Near

Painted version of a mask helmet. (*Photo and copyright by Les Guerriers du Moyen-Age*)

Ramla, the Crusaders were joined by Tancred and by Godfrey's brother, Eustace, who had been sent with some knights to capture Nablus after the fall of Jerusalem. The main army, guided by Godfrey, marched with Patriarch Arnulf at the head with the relics of the True Cross and the Holy Lance. The invading Fatimid army consisted of 20,000 men, coming from every corner of the Muslim world, and was supported by a fleet that was anchored in the port of Ascalon. The Fatimid commanders were unaware that the Crusaders were marching against them, having planned to besiege Jerusalem and retake the Holy City as soon as possible. On 11 August, upon reaching Ascalon, the Crusaders found sheep and goats gathered in the surroundings of the city to feed the nearby Fatimid camp. According to some captives taken by Tancred

Early form of great helmet. (*Photo and copyright by Les Guerriers du Moyen-Age*)

near Ramla, the animals had been left free to encourage the Crusaders to disperse for pillaging, which would have given a decisive advantage to the Fatimids. Godfrey, however, maintained order among his troops and captured the cattle without dispersing his forces. On the morning of 12 August, the day of the decisive battle, the Crusaders deployed in three main divisions: the left was commanded by Godfrey,

Decorated version of a great helmet. (*Photo and copyright by Les Guerriers du Moyen-Age*)

the centre by Tancred and the right by Raymond (having by now re-joined the rest of the Crusader army). Each division comprised of three smaller sub-divisions: one of foot soldiers marching at the front and two of knights at the rear. The clash took place not far from both Ascalon and the Fatimid camp. Although it did not last long, it was an extremely violent affair. Initially, the Fatimid vanguard was able to outflank the Crusaders and surround their rearguard, but this assault was repulsed by Godfrey. During the ensuing hand-to-hand fighting, which involved only a portion of the Muslim troops, the Fatimids suffered severe casualties, their lightly armoured troops being no match for the veteran Christian *milites*. Eventually the Fatimids panicked and fled back to the safety of Ascalon's walls, leaving the Crusaders victorious. The First Crusade, a largely Norman enterprise, thus ended in complete success.

Chapter 8

The Norman Kingdom of Sicily

Robert Guiscard, as we have seen, was a very ambitious warlord. Before his conquest of southern Italy was completed, he planned to invade the Balkan territories of the Byzantine Empire by crossing the Adriatic Sea from Apulia. After having been utterly defeated by the Seljuk Turks at the Battle of Manzikert, the Byzantines experienced serious military difficulties and their empire seemed to be on the verge of collapse. In 1081, Robert Guiscard and his son, Bohemond of Taranto, landed on the Albanian coast at the head of a large military force, which took the important city of Dyrrachium and later advanced across central Greece. The Normans obtained a series of victories during the early phase of the war, but were stopped in Thessaly by strong resistance from the Byzantines. Before they could land more troops in the Balkans, however, Robert and his son had to send most of their forces back home because Holy Roman Emperor Henry IV had been convinced by the Byzantines to attack the Norman possessions in southern Italy. Robert Guiscard died in 1085, after which the remaining Norman troops still fighting in the Balkans returned home; the menace represented by Henry IV, however, had vanished. Upon Robert Guiscard's death, the territorial possessions of the Hauteville family were inherited by Robert's younger brother, Roger (who had played a prominent role in the conquest of Sicily), and by Robert's second son, Roger Borsa. The first became Count of Sicily, while the latter became Count of Apulia and Calabria, thereby controlling all the mainland Italian territories. This division of Robert Guiscard's domains was not accepted by Robert's eldest son, Bohemond of Taranto, who rose up in revolt. The ensuing Norman civil war, however, did not last long, the Pope swiftly intervening to halt the hostilities. A compromise was found, according to which Bohemond was given some Apulian lands centred on the port city of Taranto and the title of Prince of Taranto. Bohemond, however, was never particularly enthusiastic about his new secondary role and so – when the opportunity came in 1096 – he decided to leave southern Italy and join the First Crusade with the objective of conquering a realm for himself in the Middle East. As we have seen in the previous chapter, he was able to do so thanks to the decisive support of his ambitious nephew, Tancred, who was the son of his daughter, Emma. The Principality of Antioch created by Bohemond in

Cervelliere helmet. (*Photo and copyright by Les Guerriers du Moyen-Age*)

the Levant had a distinctive Norman character from the beginning, which was lost only around 1130 when it became a vassal state of the larger Kingdom of Jerusalem.

Roger of Sicily proved to be an excellent ruler, re-Christianizing the island without using violent methods and expanding his domains in the Mediterranean by annexing Malta. Roger was always strongly supported by the papacy, having substituted the Orthodox religious prominence among the Christians of Sicily with the Catholic faith and because he always acted as a defender of the Church. Roger of Sicily died in June 1101 and was succeeded by his son, Simon, who was only a child and died

Chapel de fer helmet. (*Photo and copyright by Les Guerriers du Moyen-Age*)

four years later. As a result, another son – named Roger like his father – became the Norman ruler of Sicily as Roger II, under the regency of his mother. Roger II started to rule Sicily autonomously from 1112. Meanwhile, in continental southern Italy, Roger Borsa had died during 1111 and been replaced by his son, William II. When the latter died childless in July 1127, Roger II claimed all the continental possessions of the Hauteville family for himself. The Pope, Honorius II, was initially against Roger II's plan for the creation of a single Norman state in Italy, but was finally forced to recognize him as the Duke of Apulia. After Honorius II died in February 1130, two opposing pretenders to the papal throne emerged: Innocent and Anacletus. Roger II supported the latter in exchange for the promise that the future Pope would crown him king of southern Italy. After his candidate became Pope as Anacletus II, Roger II was indeed crowned King of Sicily in Palermo on Christmas Day 1130.

Soon after the creation of the new realm, which covered a large area and was the most prominent military power in Italy, Roger II had to face a series of internal and external threats. First, he had to crush a rebellion by the city of Amalfi, whose merchants had no intention of becoming part of a large kingdom within which their commercial supremacy over the Mediterranean would lose most of its significance. Amalfi was blockaded from the sea and forced to capitulate, after which it lost most of its economic power to the other Maritime Republics of northern Italy. Roger also had to face a series of Norman feudal rebellions, which he crushed only with difficulty and after suffering several defeats. By 1134, the internal revolts had temporarily ended, but a large anti-Norman coalition was already emerging in northern Italy, comprising Holy Roman Emperor Lothair III, the Maritime Republic of Pisa and the Byzantine Empire. In 1135, a Pisan fleet blockaded Naples and joined forces with the rebel Norman lords who rose up again in revolt. Most of Campania was temporarily occupied by the insurgents before Roger II disembarked at Salerno at the head of his royal army, which was previously stationed in Sicily. The king easily recaptured all the lands he had lost and besieged Naples, but due to health problems he was unable to take the city. Nevertheless, Naples duly returned under his control. In 1136, the imperial army of Lothair III invaded the Kingdom of Sicily and the Norman feudal lords again rose up in revolt against Roger II, who had gone back to Sicily with most of his troops. The joint forces of Lothair and the Norman insurgents obtained a series of important victories, taking the important cities of Salerno and Bari. At this point of the war, the Pope also abandoned Roger II. However, Roger was already preparing his counter-offensive. He disembarked in Calabria and retook most of Campania, this time being able to occupy Naples. He then moved to Apulia, where on 30 October 1137, his forces suffered a temporary setback at the Battle of Rignano. During 1138 and 1139, the Norman king continued campaigning in continental southern Italy, despite having been excommunicated by the new Pope, Innocent II. The Pope invaded the Kingdom of Sicily in 1139, but his forces were ambushed and almost destroyed by the Normans. Following these events, the Treaty of Mignano was signed between Innocent II and Roger II; according to which the Pope recognized the full legitimacy of the Kingdom of Sicily. In 1139 and 1140, Roger II, now free from any external menace, could finally complete the reconquest of his realm and destroy the last pockets of feudal resistance.

In 1140, to restore order and peace in a kingdom that had been ravaged by ten years of civil wars and invasions, Roger II issued a new code of laws known as the Assizes of Ariano. This invested the king and his officials with absolute powers, introduced common legislative measures for the whole of the realm (cancelling the differences existing among the various areas), reduced the authority of the often rebellious vassals and introduced a new standard coinage. In practice, with the Assizes of Ariano, Roger transformed the Kingdom of Sicily into one of feudal Europe's most centralized realms. The king established his capital at Palermo and created a multicultural court that was made up of distinguished men having different ethnic origins: Normans, Arabs and Byzantine Greeks. Roger II greatly appreciated the cultural diversity that characterized Sicily and practiced tolerance towards the

Taller version of the *chapel de fer* helmet, with shorter brim. (*Photo and copyright by Les Guerriers du Moyen-Age*)

several religious creeds existing in his realm. He hired several Byzantine and Arab functionaries who had administrative experience and made them into his most loyal collaborators. Thanks to the advice of his new Byzantine and Arab naval commanders, Roger built a large fleet that soon became the most powerful in the Mediterranean, the king wanting to use Sicily as his main base for the conquest of further lands in northern Africa and the Balkans. In 1146, the Norman fleet besieged and captured Tripoli; two years later, a larger campaign of occupation saw his forces take Sfax and several other minor urban centres located on the Tunisian coast. In just a couple of years, the Normans had conquered the whole coastline of present-day Tunisia and Tripolitania (western Libya). In 1147, while these events took place in northern

Short-sleeved hauberk of chainmail. (*Photo and copyright by Les Guerriers du Moyen-Age*)

Africa, Roger II's naval forces captured the Byzantine island of Corfu and plundered various important Byzantine coastal centres in Greece. During 1149, the Byzantines responded by retaking Corfu, but the Norman king then sent forty of his warships to pillage the suburbs of Byzantium. Over time, it became apparent that the emergence of Norman naval power in the Mediterranean represented a serious menace for both the Italian Maritime Republics and the Byzantines, as well as for the Arabs. By the time of Roger II's death in 1154, the Normans had consolidated their presence in northern Africa, the city of Tunis becoming a vassal of the Kingdom of Sicily and the whole of modern Tunisia under firm Norman control (to the point that it was named the Kingdom of Africa). Roger II was succeeded by his son, William, who had to face a major rebellion of the feudal lords soon after his ascent to the throne. The revolt – sponsored by Pope Adrian IV, Byzantine Emperor Manuel I and Holy

Detail of the iron rings making up a chainmail. (*Photo and copyright by Historia Aquitanorum*)

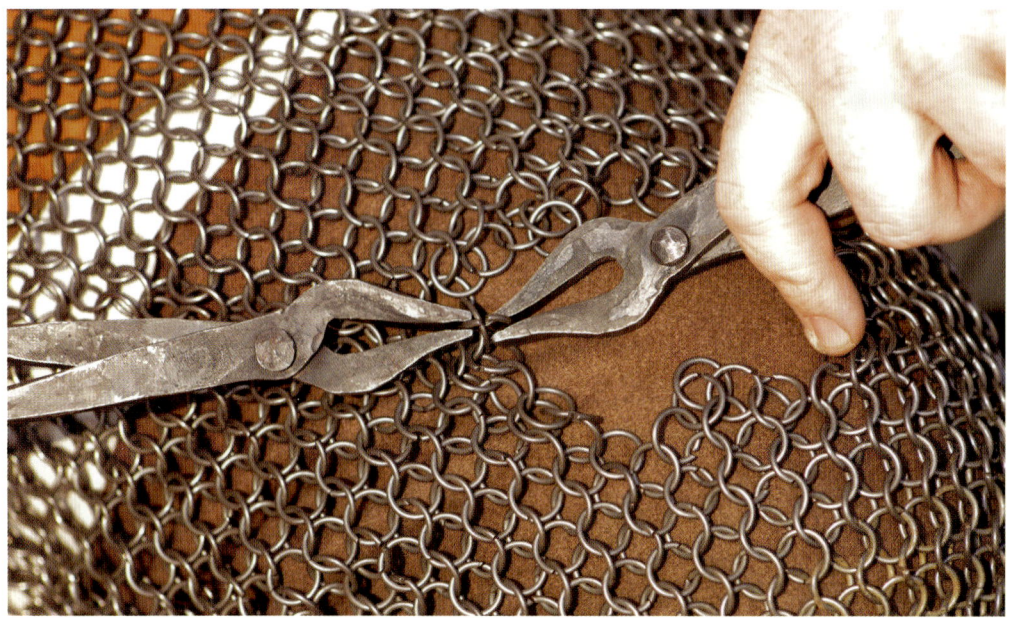

Detail showing how the rings of a chainmail could be repaired. (*Photo and copyright by Sussex Medieval Society*)

Roman Emperor Frederick Redbeard – was particularly bloody, but William was able to crush it by the end of 1156. During the uprising, the rebels of Apulia had been strongly supported by the Byzantines, so in the summer of 1157 William took his revenge on Manuel I by sending an expeditionary force of 10,000 soldiers to sack Byzantine territories in the southern Balkans. Meanwhile, in northern Africa, the situation had worsened quite rapidly for the Normans, with the ascendancy of a powerful new Muslim dynasty in Morocco (that of the Almohads) leading to the outbreak of several well-planned Arab revolts in Norman Tunisia. From 1157–60, being unable to crush the local uprisings and face a massive overland invasion by the Almohads, the Normans had no choice but to progressively abandon all their possessions in northern Africa. The brief history of the Kingdom of Africa thus came to an end. In 1160, after Tunisia was lost, King William had to face a rebellion of his nobles in Sicily and was captured by some members of his own family who wanted to dethrone him. However, the revolt soon failed when the military rallied around King William and helped him to crush the rebels.

King William died on 7 May 1166 and was succeeded by his son, William II. The new monarch married Joan, daughter of King Henry II of England, in 1177 and organized the marriage of his aunt, Constance (daughter of Roger II), and future Holy Roman Emperor Henry VI. William II, having no legitimate heir, chose Constance as his successor on the throne of Sicily, an unprecedented move in the history of his realm. In July 1174, William II had sent an army of 30,000 soldiers to Alexandria in Egypt, wishing to weaken the Ayyubid ruler of Egypt – the famous Saladin – before he could become too strong and menace the Crusader States in the Levant. His Egyptian expedition, however, quickly ended in complete failure. In 1185, following the worsening of his relations with the Byzantines, William attacked and conquered Dyrrachium in Albania, as Robert Guiscard had done more than a century before. The Norman army marched across the Balkans to Thessalonica, while the Norman fleet captured the Ionian Islands. After occupying and sacking Thessalonica, the Norman troops marched on Byzantium but were intercepted by the main Byzantine army. In the ensuing Battle of the Strymon River on 7 November 1185, the Norman invaders were soundly defeated by the Byzantines and had to withdraw. William II was forced to abandon all his newly conquered Balkan territories and signed a peace treaty with the Byzantine Empire in 1189. The Norman king died in November 1189, his death provoking the outbreak of a major succession crisis, the great majority of the Norman aristocrats having no intention of accepting Constance as their queen. With Constance's accession to the Sicilian throne, her husband and future Holy Roman Emperor Henry VI started to rule over southern Italy and annexed it to his other domains. To avoid German rule, the Norman nobles rebelled against Constance and chose Tancred of Lecce – an illegitimate nephew of Roger II – as their new monarch. In September 1190, during the Third Crusade, King Richard I (the Lionheart) of England and King Philip II of France landed in Sicily with their forces on their journey to the Levant. After taking power, Tancred had imprisoned William II's widow, Queen Joan, who was Richard's sister, and had refused to give her the money she had inherited according to King William II's will. When Richard arrived in Sicily, where the port city of Messina was the most important logistical base for the Crusaders, he demanded the release of his sister and the immediate payment of her inheritance. On 28 September, Tancred duly released Joan but did not pay the sum that Richard had called for. The presence of many English and French soldiers in Sicily added confusion to the political struggles that ravaged the Kingdom of Sicily. The population of the island saw the strangers as a potential menace and was jealous of the realm's independence. In October, the people of Messina rose up against the Crusaders and demanded that they leave their land. Richard, in order to show his military superiority to both Tancred and Philip, who were near Messina at the time, attacked the city and captured it on 4 October. After looting and burning Messina, King Richard transformed the Sicilian port into his main military base. On 4 March 1191, after several months of increasing tension and thanks to the mediation of Philip, a treaty was signed between Richard and Tancred. According to the treaty, Joan was to receive 20,000 ounces of gold as compensation

Detail showing how the spurs were worn over chainmail. (*Photo and copyright by Les Guerriers du Moyen-Age*)

for her inheritance. After these events, both Richard and Philip remained in Sicily to complete their preparations for sailing on to the Holy Land. During this period, however, tensions increased between the two monarchs, who were allies on paper only. Frequent skirmishes took place between the English and French forces, while Philip started plotting with Tancred against Richard. However, open hostilities were avoided and the Crusader kings left southern Italy in the spring of 1191.

While these events took place in Sicily, Henry VI and Constance were officially crowned Holy Roman Emperor and Holy Roman Empress in Rome in April 1191 by Pope Celestine III following Frederick Redbeard's death in the Third Crusade. The couple soon assembled a large German army and marched on the Kingdom of Sicily in an attempt to claim the realm. Initially, the imperial troops obtained a series of victories, but they soon had to stop to besiege Naples. During the investment of the city, many of the German soldiers succumbed to malaria and the invasion of southern Italy was temporarily suspended. Constance remained with a small imperial garrison in the city of Salerno, but was then captured by the local nobles – who changed sides after Henry VI left Italy with the bulk of his forces – and sent to King

Long-sleeved padded *aketon*. (*Photo and copyright by Les Guerriers du Moyen-Age*)

Tancred as a hostage. In 1192, thanks to the mediation of the Pope, Tancred released Constance in the hope that this would convince both the papacy and Henry VI to recognize him as the legitimate King of Sicily. In 1194, before a new imperial invasion of southern Italy could materialize, Tancred died of natural causes. His young son was crowned as King William III, but was placed under the regency of his mother, Sibylla, since he was still a child. In August 1194, Henry VI launched a fresh invasion of the Kingdom of Sicily, during which the whole mainland portion of the realm was swiftly occupied and the German forces then landed in Sicily. On 20 November, the Holy Roman Emperor entered Palermo and captured the young William III, who was blinded and castrated so that he could no longer represent a rival for Constance. The last Norman monarch of Sicily would die as a prisoner, in Germany, in 1198. The new Swabian dynasty that began ruling the Kingdom of Sicily in 1194 inherited a rich and flourishing realm from its Norman predecessors. Indeed, under Frederick II, son of Henry VI and Constance, southern Italy would reach the peak of its political and military power in the Middle Ages.

Chapter 9

Norman Military Organization and Equipment

Duchy of Normandy and Kingdom of England

With the Norman Conquest of 1066, feudalism was brought to the Kingdom of England from the Duchy of Normandy, King William parcelling out the lands of his new realm to the barons who had fought under him at the Battle of Hastings. According to the latest calculations, around 5,000 knights were enfeoffed – given a fiefdom – by William the Conqueror during the first phase of his reign. The English lands were not only given to lay barons, but also to clerical nobles (princes of the Church). Each baron, whether lay or clerical, was required to provide the knights who were under his orders to the king in case of war. According to the *Cartae Baronum* of 1166, a compilation of data detailing the military obligations of all English nobles, 784 knights out of 5,000 were to be provided by clerical barons. The military system based on sub-infeudation – the division of the barons' major fiefdoms into minor ones given to knights – became increasingly complex. An important military document dated 1181 – the Assize of Arms – prescribed that when the number of knights sub-infeudated within his fiefdom fell short of the knight-service owed to the monarch, a feudal tenant should maintain sufficient harness to equip some knights making up his personal household in order to make up the difference. Most of the English nobles had personal households consisting of loyal knights who provided military service in exchange for money rather than land. These retinues of professional soldiers could consist of just a few individuals or of larger contingents, depending on the wealth of the baron paying them. Compulsory military service based on the feudal military structure – known as *servitium debitum* – could last for a maximum of sixty days (later reduced to forty) after mobilization. The knights holding a fiefdom, however, were not the only professional soldiers who could be called to serve a Norman king. There were also tenants of an inferior social status, who were known as sergeants. These, despite not being nobles, had been given a land property by the monarchy in exchange for their military service. Originally the sergeants were required to serve as heavy infantrymen, since they did not have the economic resources to maintain a horse. Over time, however, some of them became rich enough to equip themselves exactly like the noble *milites*. It should be noted,

Some nice examples of Norman swords. (*Photo and copyright by Milites Pagenses*)

however, that the number of sergeants living in the Kingdom of England always remained quite small, especially if compared with those serving under the King of France.

The personal household of the monarch, known as the *familia regis*, consisted of a few hundred knights acting as the personal bodyguard of the king. These served for money and responded only to the monarch. The members of the royal household were usually organized into constabularies that had an average strength of 100 *milites stipendiarii* (paid knights). The feudal knights, instead, served in small groups of between twenty and twenty-five *milites* that were known as a *conrois* and had their own distinctive banners. A variable number of *conrois* could be assembled together to form the larger *batailles*, or battles – the cavalry divisions deployed for pitched battles. Each knight, whether feudal or mercenary, was usually accompanied on the battlefield by one or two esquires. These played only an auxiliary role and were tasked with managing the three horses owned by each *miles* – the *destrier* (war horse), the *courser* employed for travelling long distances and the *rouncey*, which transported equipment – but could also fight as light cavalry in case of emergency. The royal household, in addition to the *milites stipendiarii*, eventually started to include increasing numbers of mercenaries recruited from abroad (mostly from northern France). The Norman army that invaded England in 1066 included a sizeable number of mercenaries from

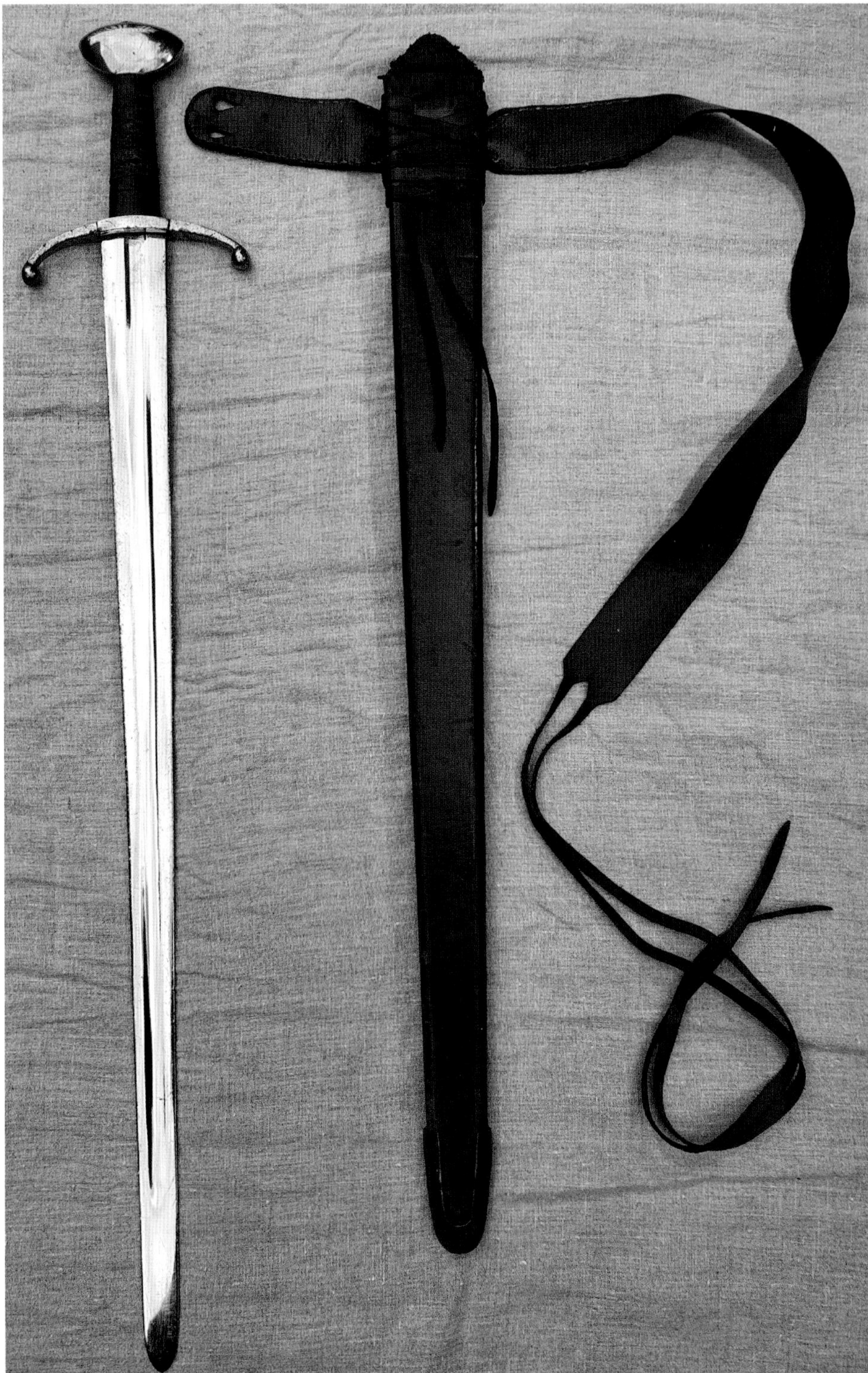

Norman sword. (*Photo and copyright by Historia Aquitanorum*)

northern France, and King William continued to recruit professional soldiers on the continent – from the French regions of Brittany, Anjou and Maine – for most of his reign. During the Anarchy period in the mid-twelfth century, both King Stephen and Empress Matilda had sizeable mercenary contingents under their orders. These mostly consisted of Welsh light infantry and Brabançon/Flemish heavy infantry. The latter were particularly appreciated, since they were the only foot soldiers of Western Europe who could resist a cavalry charge on the open field thanks to their excellent personal equipment. A standard Brabançon/Flemish infantryman was a pikeman equipped with helmet, chainmail and shield. The pikes (*geldons*) of these professional soldiers, who were extremely loyal to their employers if paid regularly, were 10–12ft long and could cause serious harm to a heavy knight. Empress Matilda, who had ruled the Holy Roman Empire for several years, fully appreciated the excellent combat skills of the mercenary Brabançon/Flemish infantry.

Cavalry was not the only component of the Norman armies, as they also included sizeable contingents of infantry. After the Norman Conquest of England, the old *fyrd* military system created by the Saxons a few centuries before was not cancelled. Under the *fyrd*, each able-bodied free man aged between 16 and 60 and living in any shire in England could be called to serve by his overlord in case of war. Those individuals who refused military service were subject to fines or the loss of their properties. A commoner, for example, had to pay a fine of 30 shillings if he neglected compulsory military service. Service in the *fyrd* was usually of short duration and had practically no costs for the royal authorities, since the members of this general levy were expected to provide their own arms and provisions and were not paid by the monarch for their military service. Originally, the *fyrd* was mobilized and organized on a local basis, according to the tribal subdivisions of the various communities, but with the arrival of the Normans and feudalism it started to be managed by the lords. Each knight could mobilize a certain number of peasants who lived and worked on his land properties in order to form a small retinue of poorly equipped infantrymen. In case of large-scale foreign invasions, it was the king's responsibility to call up the national *fyrd*, which was made up of all the able-bodied men of his realm. Conditions of service for the national *fyrd* (also known as the great *fyrd*) and for the more common shire *fyrd* were quite different, since in most cases the English peasantry were not happy about the idea of serving far from their homes for long periods of time. Most of the English freemen were peasants, who spent their lives working in the fields and following the natural cycles. As a result, on most occasions, service in the great *fyrd* could last only for very limited periods of time – sixty days, later reduced to forty – and the king had to pay his freemen if any additional period of service was needed. From the late Saxon period, a quota system of mobilization

Some nice examples of Norman swords. (*Photo and copyright by Historia Aquitanorum*)

Detail showing how the sword was attached to the waistbelt. (*Photo and copyright by Historia Aquitanorum*)

existed inside the *fyrd*; on most occasions, only one freeman from each five hides of land (a hide was an area of land that could support a peasant family, traditionally around 120 acres) was required to join the national *fyrd* when it was mobilized for a campaign. The selected individual was expected to be equipped with spear and shield, with provisions for two months and a wage of 4 shillings that were provided by the other men living on the five hides of land from which he was levied. The Norman kings abolished payments for the members of the *fyrd*, since feudal military service was considered to be a duty for each peasant, but the Plantagenets reintroduced them in the late twelfth century, including for when the peasant infantrymen were not serving abroad. During the late Saxon period, a new social class of lesser noblemen, the *thegns*, had emerged from the rural communities and had started to hold estates whose average extent was five hides. These minor landowners, after the Norman Conquest, were mostly transformed into sergeants, who were frequently employed by knights as the commanders of their feudal infantry retinues. The smallest contingents of peasant foot soldiers could be commanded by parish priests, while the largest ones were usually led by the local sheriffs – royal officials responsible for keeping the peace in the various shires and for arranging the annual shire payment owed to the king.

Kingdom of Sicily

In 1140, in front of an assembly of all the nobles of his new realm, Roger II enacted the founding laws of the Kingdom of Sicily known as the Assizes of Ariano. According to these, the power of the various Norman lords was absolute inside their own fiefdoms, but they submitted to the authority of the king for all matters regarding the general administration of the state. All the Norman aristocrats of the new realm received their lands and privileges *in capite*, by concession of the king, as a result of which the monarch was – at least formally – the sole owner of all the kingdom's territory. The king could deprive his vassals of lands and privileges at any time, if they rebelled against his rule or refused to fulfil military obligations. According to the military system adopted in 1140, the feudal forces of the Kingdom of Sicily could be mobilized in three different ways according to the military needs of the campaign: *expeditio*, *adiuvamentum regni* and *equitatura*. The *expeditio* was the usual kind of mobilization, involving only feudal troops sent by the various nobles and mostly employed for campaigns of conquest conducted outside the kingdom (whose standard duration was forty days). The *adiuvamentum regni* was the total mobilization used to face military emergencies like a foreign invasion: this involved all feudal troops of the kingdom but also non-feudal contingents (mostly made up of free men from the major cities, but also of peasants living on royal fiefdoms or around royal castles). With the *adiuvamentum regni*, all feudal lords had to send twice the number of men they were obliged to provide for an *expeditio* (this practice being known as the *augmentum*), and there was no time limit in the employment of the mobilized troops. The *equitatura* was a partial mobilization that was used to conduct small-scale local operations: it involved only the feudal forces of the area affected by the military operations and was generally used to suppress local rebellions of nobles. According to the Assizes of Ariano, all the knights of the Kingdom of Sicily were divided into two main categories: the *milites* and the *milites stipendiarii*. The former were the proper noble knights, coming from aristocratic families, whereas the latter were non-nobles who served the king as professional fighters. The term *stipendiarii* meant that they were paid for their services, but they were elite soldiers rather than simple mercenaries. In many cases, these non-noble knights were ex-Lombard or ex-Byzantine soldiers who had passed into the service of the Normans. They were mostly used to garrison royal fiefdoms and castles, or were part of the king's personal retinue (*familia regis*).

It is important to note that the Norman monarchy of Sicily employed a very precise system to determine the exact number of *milites* that each noble had to provide. Between 1150 and 1152, the realm created a register known as the *Catalogus Baronum* that listed all the military obligations of the kingdom's aristocracy. No other monarchy of Europe could count on such an important administrative document: as a result, the innovative example of the Normans was soon followed by other states during the following decades. Basically, the *Catalogus Baronum* was a list of all the vassals of the King of Sicily. In it, next to the name of each noble was an exact description of the lands and privileges owned by them and of their military obligations owed to the king. The document – similar in many aspects to William the Conqueror's Domesday Book – was constantly updated by a special office of the court known as the *Duana Baronum*. The number of knights that each vassal had to provide was calculated according to the economic revenues from the lands in his possession, the unit of measure used for this process being the *feudum integrum* (also known as the *feudum militis*). A *feudum integrum* (or full fiefdom) had an economic revenue that corresponded to 20 ounces of gold, which was considered as the standard sum of money needed to provide a good horse and full equipment to a knight. A *feudum non integrum*, instead, was a fiefdom whose value was less than 20 ounces of gold. All the minor nobles who did not hold a *feudum integrum* were obliged to unite their economic resources with those of other minor vassals in order to reach the sum of money needed to field a knight. In the Kingdom of Sicily, military service of all nobles was mandatory (*servitium personarum*) and could not be substituted with payment of an exemption (*servitium pecuniarium*).

Command of the Kingdom of Sicily's military forces was given to the counts of the realm, who had the task of supervising the military activities of the minor vassals. During military campaigns, each count was helped by a high-ranking officer nominated by the king called a *connestabile comitale*, an experienced field commander who supported his count in all aspects related to the practical conduct of operations.

From 1149, the whole Kingdom of Sicily was divided into ten military and administrative areas, known as *connestabilie*, each of which was under the orders of a senior military officer, nominated by the king and called a *connestabile regio*. In the event of an *adiuvamentum regni*, each of these officers was responsible for assembling and leading the non-feudal military forces raised from royal fiefdoms. In addition to knights, the various feudal lords listed in the *Catalogus Baronum* also had to provide a fixed number of auxiliary soldiers, which was calculated with the same principles used to determine the number of knights. The auxiliary soldiers could belong to three different categories: *servientes*, *pedites* and *balistarii*. The *servientes* were the squires of the heavily armed knights, who served in the royal army as light cavalry, whereas the *pedites* and *balistarii* were the retainers who followed their feudal lords during a military campaign. The *pedites* were regular infantrymen, mostly armed with spears, while the *balistarii* were equipped as archers. The military forces of the Kingdom of Sicily also included the powerful *familia regis*, or royal household, a small private army

The points of two Norman spears. The model on the right, with two small wings, was used for thrusting in close combat, while the other was preferred for throwing. (*Photo and copyright by Historia Aquitanorum*)

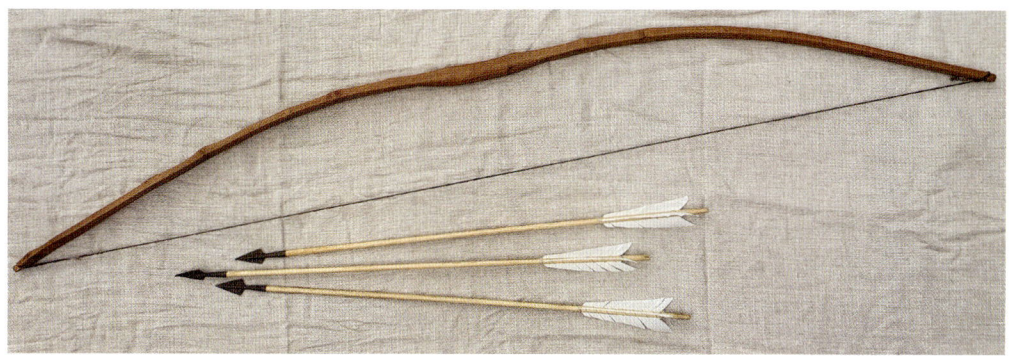

Norman bow and arrows. (*Photo and copyright by Historia Aquitanorum*)

placed under the direct control of the king. Its core was represented by a number of elite professional knights (*milites stipendiarii*), who had strong personal relations with the monarch and whose loyalty to the crown was absolute. Commanded by an officer known as the *maestro connestabile*, the *familia regis* also included a large number of Arab mercenary infantrymen or archers from Sicily or Tunisia. The first Norman king to employ Arab mercenaries was Roger II, who considered them to be the most loyal and valorous of all his soldiers. Being foreigners, they had no links with the political intrigues of the Norman aristocracy and thus could be employed to put down any plot organized against the royal family.

Equipment

The Norman *milites* of the period covered in this book were all protected by a hauberk, or shirt of chainmail, which was made of several thousand interlocking metal rings. The dimensions of each hauberk could vary considerably, since the sleeves could reach only to the elbow or be full arm-length. The bottom of the hauberk generally reached the knees, but could be longer or shorter. Producing this kind of armour was a long and costly process, which only nobles could sustain, yet despite this, the diffusion of chainmail among knights was practically universal. By the mid-twelfth century, the personal protection of a knight also included various other elements made of chainmail, including *chausses* (armour protecting the legs) and gloves. At that time, separate hoods of chainmail for protection of the head were not yet in use, the portion of chainmail protecting the head and neck simply being part of the hauberk. The chainmail was worn over a padded garment known as the *aketon*, which offered additional protection to its wearer. The Norman knights of the Kingdom of Sicily and those who participated in military campaigns in the Byzantine Empire or in the Holy Land sometimes replaced their hauberks with

Quiver of a Norman bow. (*Photo and copyright by Milites Pagenses*)

Norman Military Organization and Equipment 145

Norman crossbow with darts. (*Photo and copyright by Historia Aquitanorum*)

local models of scale armour, but these never became popular in southern Italy. The standard headgear of the Norman knights was the conical helmet with nasal, but over time a semi-spherical version with full facial mask became increasingly common. The skull of a nasal helmet could be made from a single sheet of iron or be of composite construction. The nasal was fully integrated into either the skull or brow of the helmet; it was usually riveted to the skull or was part of a T-shaped piece protecting both the nose and the eyebrows. During the twelfth century, the skull of the nasal helmet became more varied: it could have a forward-deflected apex (resembling the shape of a Phrygian cap) or could be round-topped. During the late twelfth century, due to the increasing use of the crossbow on European battlefields, most of the knights started to abandon their previous helmets with no protection for the face (except for the nasal) and replaced them with new ones having different patterns of facial masks. The latter were fixed and gave protection only to the frontal part of the face. The standard shield of the Norman *milites* was the kite shield, which was specifically designed for cavalry use and gave a high degree of protection to its user. Almond-shaped, it was made of laminated wood and was covered with stretched animal hide that could be painted in different decorative motifs. A band of metal was placed on the external edge of the shield for reinforcement, and to protect the handle on the reverse, each kite shield had a round metal reinforcement on the front known as the umbo (a boss that could be pointed in order to be used as an offensive weapon during close combat). Kite shields were usually equipped with *enarmes* (leather gripping straps) on their back, which gripped them tightly to the arm even when their users relaxed their arms. They also had an additional long strap that allowed them to be slung over the shoulder when not in use. The standard dimensions of a kite shield corresponded to the approximate space between a horse's neck and its rider's thigh; the narrow bottom of the shield protected the rider's left leg and the pronounced upper curve protected both the left shoulder and torso of the rider. Due to these peculiar features, the kite shield was perfect for cavalry use, being much more effective than the previous round shield.

The main offensive weapons of the Norman knights were the spear and the longsword. Norman spears were produced in two main versions: throwing and thrusting spears. The heads of throwing spears had an average length of 20cm, while thrusting spears had a standard length of 70cm. Spear heads consisted of two parts: the blade and the socket. The wooden shaft was fixed into the socket with one or two nails; sometimes spears could also have two projections on the side of the socket, known as wings, which were used to remove the spear more easily from enemy shields. Occasionally, the back end of the shaft was capped with a metal ferrule. Spear blades could be of two different kinds, the older of which was forged with a herringbone pattern along the middle and had curved edges, blending inconspicuously into the socket. The second model of blade had nearly straight edges (which ended in an angle at the base) and a marked narrowing as it merged into the socket. Wings were very common on the first model but quite rare on the second. They had another important practical function in addition to easing the extraction of the spear from enemy shields: they could be used for hooking onto the edge of an enemy shield and thus opening the way for a strike at the opponent. The wooden shaft of the thrusting spear was longer than that of the throwing spear – 2.5–3m compared to 1.5m. The diameter of all shafts was about 2.5cm, and they sometimes narrowed towards the back end. Throwing spears were less popular than thrusting ones, as the Normans were the first knights in feudal Europe to start using their spears tucked under the armpit during frontal charges. Thanks to the employment of stirrups and solid saddles with tall pommels, the Norman *milites* could remain stable on their horses while thrusting with the spears placed under their armpits. Before the widespread adoption of stirrups, the cavalry of Antiquity wielded their spears overarm, so could not thrust them with great power. Swords were much more expensive and complex to produce than spears. The Norman sword was a single-handed weapon that was designed to leave one of the warrior's hands free in order to hold the shield. Their hilt consisted of three parts: back-hilt, grip and fore-hilt. Sometimes, the latter was made up of two parts, the hindmost one of which was commonly known as the pommel. Most of the hilts were made of iron, but sometimes they could be of bronze. The total length of a Norman sword was of 90–95cm, while the average length of the blade was 75–80cm. Blades were 5–6cm wide and their weight was restricted towards the point, which was caused by tapering them both in breadth and thickness. In consequence, blade thickness was 6mm near the hilt and just 2mm at the point of the sword. To reduce the weight further and to increase flexibility, a groove was forged and ground out along the middle of the blade. The centre of gravity of the weapon was near the hilt, which made it quite easy to handle. Many swords, especially those belonging to the richest men, had decorative inscriptions on the blade and decorated hilts. All swords were carried in leather-bound wooden scabbards that were often suspended from a strap across the right shoulder. Like the scabbard, the hilt was also made of an organic material such as horn or antler.

The poorest feudal infantrymen had no military equipment to speak of: they went to war wearing their ordinary clothes and were mostly armed with their agricultural tools. A fortunate few had a padded *aketon* and a simple helmet (usually of conical shape). The foot sergeants and the mercenary infantrymen from the continent were much better equipped than the peasant levies, all having helmets and frequently wearing a full chainmail over their *aketon*. Some of them even had *chausses*, while almost all were armed with long pikes that had to be used with both hands. The quilted *aketon* – the armour of the poor – was also popular among the archers. It was usually made of linen or wool, with the stuffing being obtained from materials like scrap cloth or horsehair. Quilted hoods for protection of the head were usually worn together with the *aketon*. The archers of the Norman period were equipped with bows made from yew, ash or elm, which had a draw force of 100lb and an effective range of 200m. Technically, they should be called longbows because they were made from a single piece of wood. The overall height of a Norman bow generally corresponded to that of its user. When not in use, a Norman bow was almost straight; when strung,

The personal equipment of a Norman crossbowman. (*Photo and copyright by Les Guerriers du Moyen-Age*)

Norman hunting horn, also used on the battlefield to transmit orders. (*Photo and copyright by Milites Pagenses*)

it was nearly D-shaped in cross-section. Arrowheads could be of three different kinds: blade-shaped, spike-shaped and chisel-shaped. Spike-shaped arrowheads were specifically designed for combat use, the other two also being employed for hunting. Each arrowhead was fixed with a tang to its shaft; this was made of wood, had feathers applied on the back and was 65–75cm long.

Bibliography

Bartlett, R., *England under the Norman and Angevin Kings 1075–1225* (Oxford University Press, 2003).
Cuozzo, E., *La cavalleria nel regno Normanno di Sicilia* (Mephite, 2009).
D'Amato, R. and Salimbeti, A., *The Normans in Italy 1016–1194* (Osprey Publishing, 2020).
Gravett, C., *Norman Knight 950–1204* (Osprey Publishing, 1994).
Grillo, P., *Cavalieri e popoli in armi. Le istituzioni militari nell'Italia medievale* (Laterza, 2014).
Green, J.A., *Henry I: King of England and Duke of Normandy* (Cambridge University Press, 2009).
Heath, I., *Armies of Feudal Europe 1066–1300* (Wargames Research Group, 1989).
Heath, I., *Armies of the Dark Ages 600–1066* (Wargames Research Group, 1980).
Nicolle, D., *French Medieval Armies 1000–1300* (Osprey Publishing, 1991).
Nicolle, D., *Italian Medieval Armies 1000–1300* (Osprey Publishing, 2002).
Nicolle, D., *The Normans* (Osprey Publishing, 1987).
Spencer, C., *The White Ship: Conquest, Anarchy and the Wrecking of Henry I's Dream* (William Collins, 2020).
Wise, T., *Saxon, Viking and Norman* (Osprey Publishing, 1979).

The Re-enactors who Contributed to this Book

Historia Aquitanorum
Historia Aquitanorum is a French living history association, whose purpose is to reconstitute both civilian and military daily life of the second half of the twelfth century in a Seigniory located in the Dukedom of Aquitaine. Our main goal is to get as close as possible to the historical facts so as to help people discover this unknown or rather little-known period. To achieve this, all our diverse achievements come from serious research in various domains such as iconography (illuminations, sculptures and frescoes), texts (cartularies, literary sources) and last but not least archaeological sources. We make people aware of this period through true-to-life historical characters and thematic workshops during medieval celebrations or historical recreations. We have already taken part in film shootings and TV programmes. We also organize the gatherings of various troops similar to ours from all over France and even further afield (Battle of Malemort, L'Epée et le Bourdon). You can easily contact us to check our availability and to decide about what would be best for your project. Send us an e-mail; we would be pleased to share our knowledge and our passion.

Contacts:
E-mail: info@historia-aquitanorum.fr
Website: https://www.historia-aquitanorum.fr
Facebook: https://www.facebook.com/Historia-Aquitanorum-644585265732379/

De Gueules et d'Argent
De Gueules et d'Argent is a living history group based in France. It seeks to reconstitute the troop of a *chatelaine* living in the county of Savoy at the pivotal time of the end of the twelfth century and the beginning of the thirteenth century. The group also practises the Historical European Martial Arts, with feudal individual (duelling) and group combat. Nathanaël Dos Reis, leader of the group, is a historian preparing a PhD thesis on the evolution of the military equipment of the equestrian fighter from the eleventh to the thirteenth century.

Contacts:
E-mail: degueulesetdargent@gmail.com and nathanaeldosreis.culture@gmail.com
Facebook: https://www.facebook.com/degueulesetdargent

Milites Pagenses

Milites Pagenses is a small Breton association of historical reconstitution working on the first decades of the twelfth century. The heart of our work is the evocation of the household of a knight and of peasant feudal levies from this historical period.

Contacts:
Website: https://militespagenses.jimdofree.com/
Facebook: https://www.facebook.com/MilitesPagenses

Sussex Medieval Society

As a living history association, we strive to portray an authentic impression of Anglo-Norman military and civilian life between the years 1066 and 1267. Our period is rich with history, starting with the Norman invasion and conquest of England in 1066 after Harold's defeat at the Battle of Hastings. Following this there was a period of constant conflict and instability, with the Harrowing of the North, the Anarchy and the First and Second Barons' Wars all within the following two centuries. Our civilian camps include authentic examples of contemporary cooking, woodwork, *maille* work and leatherwork, to name but a few. When in the field, we use techniques and manuals from our period to engage in limited and full contact combat with a huge variety of authentic medieval weaponry. We are further planning to expand into medieval music and archery over the coming years. The group was founded in May 2022 by a group of like-minded friends, all sharing a passion for things medieval. We like to think we have something for everyone, and this shows in the broad demographic that constitutes our membership. We are primarily based in Lewes, East Sussex and Portsmouth, Hampshire, although we have members from across the whole of the UK. We train every Sunday, so do not hesitate to reach out to us or pop along for a chat if this sounds like something you would enjoy!

Contacts:
E-mail: sussexmedieval@outlook.com
Website: https://www.sussexmedieval.co.uk/
Facebook: https://www.facebook.com/SussexMedieval/

Les Guerriers du Moyen-Age

The Les Guerriers du Moyen-Age association is a French historical reconstruction association created in 2001, focusing on civil and military life from the end of the twelfth century to the end of the thirteenth century. Regarding the twelfth century, the project concerns the hospital of Saint Jean de Jerusalem. Concerning the thirteenth century, the association recreates a bourgeois militia of 1274 organized and ruled in Saint-Maur-des-Fossés (near Paris). Our association also includes a section of Historical European Martial Arts focused on military combat on foot from the thirteenth century to the beginning of the fourteenth century.

Contacts:
Email: gma@guerriersma.com
Website: www.guerriersma.com
Facebook: https://www.facebook.com/GMA.reconstitution/

Index

Adrian IV, 128
Aethelred the Unready, 25
Alfred the Great, 6
Anacletus II, 125
Arnulf of Flanders, 24

Baldwin V of Flanders, 31

Charles the Simple, 20–1
Cnut the Great, 25
Constance of Hauteville, 130–3

Gilbert Drengot, 79

Harthacnut, 25
Henry VI, 130–3
Honorius II, 125

Louis the Pious, 7–8

Malcolm I of Scotland, 54–5
Malcolm III of Scotland, 60–2

Queen Joan, 130–1

Ragnar Lodbrok, 8
Rainulf of Aquitaine, 14
Ralph de Gael, 54
Ranulf Drengot, 79–80
Roger Borsa, 123–5
Roger de Breteuil, 54
Rollo, 15, 20, 22, 24
Rorik of Dorestad, 20

Sweyn II of Denmark, 49

Tancred of Lecce, 131–3
Tostig Godwinson, 32, 35, 39

William Adelin, 66, 69
William Clito, 66, 71
William Longsword, 21, 24